THE FALL
OF AMERICA

BY
ELIJAH MUHAMMAD
Messenger of Allah,
Leader and Teacher
to The American So -called Negro

Published by
MUHAMMAD'S TEMPLE OF ISLAM No. 2
7351 Stony Island Avenue
Chicago, Illinois 60649

Appreciation

In the name of Almighty Allah, the Most Merciful Saviour, Our Deliverer, Master of the Day of Judgment. To Allah alone do I submit and seek refuge.

This book was made from speeches and articles I prepared over several years.

Thanks to my staff of secretaries who have put my words on paper. Thanks to Allah for His blessings of a composing room staff of brothers, Charlie Lee X Hinton, Gene X Walton, James 90X Moore, Michael 10X Johnson, Ozie X Jones, Paul 9X Hollis, Robert 46X Hall and Sisters Gladys Bosstan and Yvonne A. X Hurst, and their many fine helpers who prepared the typesetting copy for the printers from our very own modern composing room.

To Mrs. Phyllis Burton and Miss. Yolande T. Robbins, I am grateful for their help in proofreading. Thanks to brother Eugene Majied for his art work and helpful assistance in work preparation. Finally, thanks to brother John Ali who drew together all of the efforts of those who ably assisted in the publishing of this book. Many thanks. May the peace and blessings of Allah be upon all those mentioned and the others unmentioned whose part in making this book is as major as the rest.

Elijah Muhammad,
Messenger of Allah

Introduction

The time is now for a full and clear statement of what The Honorable Elijah Muhammad is teaching, what he is about, why he is doing it and why nothing will stop his forward action.

First, let it be said that he is not a racist. Unlike the white race, he does not preach the inferiority of any race or group. He does not advocate denial of any group's rights and categorically asserts that every citizen has the right, (should he wish to use it), to exert the rights of citizenship offered him.

Either through ignorance or evil intent, some have confused racism with religious dogma.

Mr. Elijah Muhammad teaches that the so-called American Negroes are the chosen of Allah. He teaches that all others are among the non-chosen and nothing they can do will alter that fact. This is the grounds on which so many accuse him of racism. If this be racism, then every religion since man has preached racism.

The Jews teach that they are Jehovah's elect. The entire sequence of events that culminated in the death of the man called Jesus was set in action because he, Jesus, sought to destroy the concept of the elect.

The Catholic church teaches that it is the only church. It forbids its members to intermarry with non Catholics, save under special dispensations and even then the children of such marriages must be pledged to the Church before the marriage takes place. Catholics are taught not to consort with non-Catholics in religious terms of reference.

The Baptist church teaches that it alone is right, that

Christians who have not been submerged under the water have not received true salvation.

Admittedly, each of these groups teaches a doctrine that tells its followers that they are the elect, that they are set apart and that their spiritual insight is the only one worth holding. So does Mr. Elijah Muhammad.

Mr. Muhammad says we are the elect of Allah in the same sense that a Jew says he is the elect of Jehovah or that other denominations pursue their theological ends.

If Mr. Muhammad in teaching Islam is accused of racism, then so must every other religious denomination or sect.

Much is made of the fact that Mr. Muhammad predicts the early end of the non-Muslims. This is what he believes. This is what he knows. This is what he teaches. If he is wrong, then it is a matter between him and His Teacher. But again, the truth of history is on his side.

The New Testament is laced with promises that the non-Christians will be destroyed in a fiery death, soon to come.

Were one to take the time to trace through an elementary course in comparative religion, it would be abundantly clear that every religion has felt its enemies would meet with destruction, and very soon at that. Why the uproar when Mr. Muhammad teaches Black men that they are the elect and that their opponents will soon be destroyed?

Attacks on Mr. Muhammad have centered around the charge that he and his followers are a cult, a non-religious group. Proponents of this lie say we are actually a racist outfit set on the destruction of the white man.

This of course is not true.

Empires in scripture and political history have risen up over the time of man and have fallen. These empires, the Romans and their Caesars, the Prussians and their Kaisers, the Russians and their Czars, the Egyptians and their Pharoahs, the Europeans and their Kings, the Turks and their Sultans and now the States of America and their Presidents. Whatever the name of the empire or the title of the ruler, it was only a grand, clever, psychological trick to dupe the naive masses then and now, especially the Black man of America, from recognizing America as Babylon. The wolf in sheep's clothing, Babylon, is in fact America today. The time has now come for the revealing of the greatest empire of Babylonian type ever to exist. No nation, no empire before fits the description of Babylon as the United States or of the Babylon ruler as the rulers of America.

Mr. Elijah Muhammad is bringing a final truth to the people. He is revealing the secret of the symbols, parables, signs and prophecies of the scriptures. The Old Testament is a book of prophecy in parables, symbols and signs. The New Testament is a fulfillment of a prophecy whose time is now. All religions have talked of a doomsday, judgment day or a type of hell filled with fire and brimstone.

Despite America's skill, abundance, technology, materialism, psychology, tricknology and ability to synthesize—that great ability of making false appear true or real is well known. America can make man made fibers appear to be wool, butter that never saw a cow or fruit jam that does not come from fruit trees. Mr. Elijah Muhammad in **The Fall of America** brings us to the truth, the fateful destiny of America.

America has been a country whose leaders' pride has been to refer to it as the greatest country on earth. Babylon, the most powerful country who has as its greatest ambition to be the most armed. More than thirty-five per cent of its national budget is set aside for military preparation. America boasts of its stockpile of weapons with its great kill capacity.

The Honorable Elijah Muhammad is a man whose words will hold a high place in history. His words are clear. His is a vivid example of the voice crying in the wilderness for justice. His is the ability to read the handwriting on the wall as only Daniel could do despite Belchazzar and his scholars' highest institutional learning.

Mr. Muhammad's brilliance of style and accuracy of statement are perfectly compatible in an historian. **The Fall of America** offers a new interpretation of the American world which is open to attack by critics, theologians, scientists, historians and anthropologists. Mr. Elijah Muhammad challenges the contemporaries of today as Moses threw down his rod as a challenge to Pharoah of Egypt. He contends that the interpretations of the scriptures, the Bible and the Holy Qur'an, are important interrelators pertaining to sequences of events leading to the resurrection of the American so-called Negro.

Mr. Muhammad shows how events of yesterday and today are the life styles depicted in symbols, signs, parables, and prophecies of history and scriptures.

VII

The ancient Orient, classical Greece, India, Islam and Europe previously had their terms. The rise of America to global pre-eminence in modern times therefore appears as the last of a long series of drastic cultural explosions leading to that long awaited final judgment called by the corrupt as "doomsday" as it is their complete end engulfed in a holocaust. Called by the abused, "judgment day," as they are now given a long deprived justice.

An important feature of **The Fall of America** is the use of non-literary sources, unchallenged, not disproved, being chosen to symbolize, depict and express trends, movements and growth of the falling American civilization.

The Fall of America is the accurate picture of history and scripture's greatest empire and its community. Such synthesis offers a new and remarkably persuasive pattern for understanding America today. There is no other Babylon. America's rapid decline of morals and spirtualism has led it to the abyss and spiralling decline whose time has come.

If the justice and spiritual aspects of scriptures are true, and they are, then America too must pay! If there is natural law of justice or compensation, justice must be given and America must pay. **The Fall of America** by Mr. Elijah Muhammad clears up all doubts.

Let this suffice as a reply to the detractors who say Mr. Elijah Muhammad and his followers are not of a true religion.

These matters being laid on the record, let us now turn to the essence today. The Black man in America is no longer willing to listen to misguided teachings of his modern-day elders called Uncle Toms. This is why the Uncle Toms are disturbed. This is why their white masters are concerned.

And well they might be, for the day when the Black man of America will scratch where they don't itch and laugh, when they are being kicked, is over.

This is why The Honorable Elijah Muhammad in teaching Islam to the Black man of America is under attack. This is why his theological teachings are being distorted into racism. This is why he and his followers who have converted to Islam are being denied the right to worship in their own manner, a right given persons of other faiths.

The crux of the matter is: the Black man of America is hungry for the leadership Mr. Muhammad so ably offers. The Black man of America is looking for more than legalisms. The Black man of America wants more than a gradual restoration of his right.

What the Black man of America seeks is a restoration of his identity as an elect people; what the Black man of America seeks is a return to his own which includes his people, his God, his religion, his language, his part of the earth, and a physical and spiritual reunion with his own nation.

But it must be admitted that even more deplorable than the attacks from the white race are the deeds and utterances of other Black men who claim love for the unity of Black man but actually through ignorance, or love of the enemy of the Black man, they are helping the cause of disunity.

In his visit to some of the governments of Islam, Mr. Muhammad received the greatest respect and honor of any so-called American Negro ever to visit that world from America. He was shown through their mills, government facilities, farms, canals, irrigation systems, new projects and Mosques. He was welcomed by all and praised for his work of freedom, justice, equality and Islam for his American Black people.

While the sound and fury explode among the so-called leaders of Black people in America, the real problem goes unattended. It is to that problem that Mr. Muhammad is dedicated and sets forth the solution in **The Fall of America.**

The Black man must be awakened from his North American slumber and be made to realize his true nature, his true God, his true name, his true religion, and his inescapable destiny.

America's world is floating in corruption; its complete disintegration is both imminent and inescapable. Any man who integrates with that world must share in its disintegration and its destruction.

If the Black man of America would but listen, he need not be a part of this certain doom.

If the Black man will listen, Mr. Muhammad will do his best to teach him.

John Ali
Chicago, Illinois
January, 1973

CONTENTS

CONTENTS

CONTENTS

CHAPTER 1

Washington, D.C. Speech May 29, 1959

(The following are excerpts from a speech I delivered before a gathering of well over ten thousand people at the Uline Arena, Washington, D.C., Sunday, May 29, 1959.)

My people, I am here to fulfill a promise made long ago. I am here to bring you the truth. I am here with a solution to the problems of the so-called Negro and his white slavemasters.

You are seeking something. You are seeking an answer to your four hundred year old problem of slavery, servitude and fifth - class citizenship. I am here with the solution to that problem. How good it is, then, for Black brothers of like minds and similar burdens to get together for a spiritual feast.

For more than four hundred years your pleas for justice, freedom, equality, a decent place in the sun have reverberated like thunderclaps sounding in the dark valleys of Lebanon. Yet there has been no answer.

Never in the history of human evil have so many asked for a just pittance, so loud, so long and received in return so little, if anything at all.

The church has failed you. Christianity has failed you. The government of America has failed you. You have not received justice from any quarter. As prophesied, you, my fellow Black men, are as sheep among wolves and, as is to be expected, every wolf is taking a bite at you. You approach the Senate, the House, the White House, and you ask for justice. You get injustice.

All our prayers have come to naught because we

have proceeded out of ignorance. We have not known the true God. We have not known who are our brothers. We have not known who are our enemies. We have not known who is God; nor have we known who is the devil. In a nutshell, we have not known the truth about God, the devil and until that truth is made plain to us, our prayers for justice will forever go unanswered. We will be the subject of scorn and laughter.

By now it should be ever so clear that politics will no more solve our problem than it did the difficulties facing Israel during her bondage in Egypt.

We have come to the brink of extinction. We must now and here make an agonizing reappraisal of our way of life if we care anything for ourselves, our lives, our people, our race, the future of our properties, wives and children.

Justice is a common thing. Yet, it is elusive. Men have sought its meaning and substance since time began. Plato shrugged that justice was nothing more than the wish of the strongest members of society. Jesus equated justice with brotherhood. Shakespeare saw it as a matter of mercy. I am here to tell you that justice is the eventual working out of the will of God as indicated in the fundamental principles of truth. Justice is the antithesis of wrong, the weapon God will use to bring judgment upon the world, the purpose and consummation of His coming.

Although we are the chosen of God, when it comes to justice, the so-called American Negroes are the most deprived people on the planet earth. Had justice prevailed, there would be no need for a day of judgment to come today, to plead, not to the unjust judges of the world, but to the just judge to give the Black man of America justice. That just judge is Allah, God. We have come to the end of the days of the unjust judges. Even though it may offend some, you must know the truth of it all.

The truth hurts the guilty. According to the sayings of Jesus, the truth will make us free. The imperative need is for a clear cut definition of that truth that will make us free. We must distinguish between the truth and the false so-called truths that have been handed down to us from generation by our slavemasters.

We have been falsely taught that the truth was the matter of Jesus' birth and death. It has been taught, and this is also false, that the truth is the revelation of Christianity. Neither of these is the truth. Neither of these will make you free.

The truth to freedom is the knowledge of God and the devil, truth of yourselves, others and the real religion of God.

How mistaken you are to assume that Jesus was the final word of truth. Jesus Himself admitted He could not tell it all. Yet He promised that God would send one who would not only reveal the ultimate truth but Who would reveal it to the people lying in the mud of ignorance and shame. We, the fools of the world, would be the first to know that truth, not the wise of this world. This is not cause for offense; for when God said He would reveal his truth to the fools of the world, it was a blessing, not an insult to us. After all, this names us His chosen people.

Thus it is that the problem of the Black man in America has set off an era of troubling throughout the world. Until your problem is solved there will not be peace for anyone. Today, then, is a new day dawning in a new world; for the old day and the old world have passed away.

The new day, the new world, if you please, cannot come into full meaning until justice comes to our people. The burden is not our oppressor's alone. Much of it is upon us. The time has come when we must speak or die. Our leaders, or so-called leaders, are choked by fear. Such a leader is not worth the salt that leavens his bread.

This fear is the root of their failure to tell you the truth. Now this truth must come out. You have misunderstood the Bible. Christianity is a white man's religion and it contains no salvation for the Black man. For this very reason, the prayers of your preachers to the government, the Father, the Son and the Holy Ghost have fallen on deaf ears.

Now, I ask you, what good is Christianity to you and to me if that religion and the God of that religion will not defend us against lynching and rape? Indeed, we would be fools to believe and trust such a religion and such a God knowing that He bestows all His blessings upon our enemy.

We are taught to look forward to a salvation that does not exist. Christianity offers you salvation after death. You must go down into the earth and rot. That kind of salvation I don't want. I will not give you two cents for it. Any man that will work hard all his life praying to God to take and give him a home beyond the grave is a fool. I am sorry if you think ill of me, but the truth is all I am going to speak. The Black man in America is in a terrible condition. He is emasculated, blinded, confused, and wandering about at high noon on judgment day. If judgment day were not here, instead of some remote hour to come, I would not be bringing you this message at this hour! Elijah is here because the day of judgment is here!

What a sorry spectacle we make before God and the nations of the world! Here we are, upwards of twenty million Black Americans who have given their blood, sweat, and service for four hundred years in the vain hope that one day justice would be ours. When the bugle call of war sounded, the Black soldier stood erect. The plains of Europe, Asia, Africa and America have been fertilized by his blood. Yet the government of the nation, for which he fought and in whose cause he died, allows his sons to be lynched and then adds salt to the wound by concealing the identity of the lynchers. More, the government seeks out the lynchers and then turns them over to their fellowmen who share the lynchers' cause and motives.

Our daughters and wives are lynched before our eyes. The government will not put a stop to it. They will allow the lynchers to lynch you and me if we are charged with an attempt to rape one of them.

The lynchers live right next door, down the street, up the alley. Yet, they are not brought to justice. All of this grief you and I must suffer. All these burdens, we must bear. It is beyond comprehension that the American government — mistress of the seas, lord of the air, conqueror of outer space, squire of the land and prowler of the deep bottoms of the oceans — is unable to defend us from assault, rape and murder on the streets of these concrete jungles. What sane man can deny that it is now time that you and I take counsel among ourselves to the end of finding justice for ourselves.

If we continue to accept these injustices, we are nothing but cowards. If we be cowards, then we ought to go home, kill our wives and then commit suicide.

We killed the devil in Germany. We killed his brothers for him. We killed our own brothers for him. Yet, we are without justice. We have nothing. Our sons and daughters are lynched, kicked, beaten, hung up in the sun, drowned in the river, in ponds and lakes. Their bodies are found in the street, on the highway, in the bushes — killed by the very people for whom they have slaved their lives out to give comfort.

When you stand up and speak a word in behalf of your own people, you are classified as a troublemaker, you are classified as a Communist, as a race hater and everything but good. How can you as a people ever be anything if you are going to crush out your leaders who try to seek justice for you even at the cost of their own lives? I, Elijah Muhammad, am classified as a race hater. What race? What teaching am I uttering that you can classify as race hatred? How can the devil say little Elijah Muhammad is teaching race hatred in the face of over four hundred years of his hatred of you and me! If God has revealed to me the truth of this race of people and yourself, and I tell you of it, and that is the truth, then don't say that I am teaching race hatred. Just say I teach the truth.

There is only one thing that I am teaching today that is hatred. That is the truth of the devil. That truth I did not know. Only God knows the truth of the devil. He has revealed it to me. If that is not the truth, let the devil attack God. It is just that the truth has come to you, people without the knowledge of the truth, the deceived, and misled by a wise, wicked scientist. I am here with the truth from God Almighty, and for that truth I will give my life. I will not hide that truth to the inducement of falsehood. I won't mix it up with falsehood. I say to you, my beloved brothers and sisters of injustice, if you will only reflect on what is said from the mouth of Elijah, you will not take it for insult. You will not take him for a race hater. You will take him for a beloved brother, a beloved teacher and a beloved defender of yourself. I am not before you of myself. I have not been sent of myself. My mission is not for me, nor is my mission from the devil. I have been sent by Almighty God, Allah. It is a very strong and powerful mission that will bring a turning point in the history of the world at large, the Black man in particular.

The truth will make you free. What is that truth that will free us? You say, "We are already free. Abraham Lincoln freed us." That is not the kind of freedom of which I speak. Abraham Lincoln was not instrumental in trying to free you. Remember that! Abraham Lincoln wanted a United States of America. They didn't want two presidents. They didn't want two governments ruling America. They wanted only one government with one president for all. It was not that they were so full of love for the so-called Negroes, that he wanted to free them from the hands of his brother. But this was a good weapon to bring his brother into submission to his idea of a United States and one President of that United States. So, therefore you were just lucky that you got freed from servitude and slavery at that time. Otherwise, you would probably still have been in servitude and slavery today. You say you love Lincoln. You love him because he freed us. He is your emancipator. I say to you, my beloved brothers and sisters, Mr. Lincoln was not your brother. He was not your friend anymore than George Washington.

Now we are one hundred years up from slavery Many of you feel proud that you have been schooled. You have a few diplomas and degrees. You can do little things educationally, but that does not get you justice in America. You still suffer injustice with an armful of diplomas and degrees from colleges and universities. Is that right? If that is not right, I am willing that you shoot me down, cut me down, anyway you please to get rid of me, if I am not right. If I am right, be aware!

What we want today is justice. We want the truth. The truth has come to you. You are not accepting it. Think it over! Here are a few of us who have accepted God to be our Lord. We have accepted Islam to be our religion — an old religion, as old as God, Himself; a religion of the prophets, of all the righteous; a religion of freedom, justice and equality; a religion of universal brotherhood; a religion that a brother will fight and die for his brother; a religion that believes in the law that was given to Moses, an eye for an eye and a tooth for a tooth!

Look at Christianity. That law is killed. Why? Because the devil did not want you to strike back at him. Therefore, they condemned an eye for an eye and a tooth for a tooth in their Christian religion because twenty million so-called Negroes might get an eye for an eye. That is nothing but the common law of justice. If you pluck out my eye, I should try and pluck out yours. But you have been made such harmless slaves by the teaching of a slavery religion called Christianity which teaches you to love, not to strike back, but to turn the other cheek. It teaches you to give freedom to the robber. If he takes one's coat then give him the cloak also. Help the robber to rob. Enrich the thief. That is the kind of religion that you are taught to believe. That is God's religion? I say my friends, it is a slavery teaching! It is against the very nature of you and me to stand and let someone smite us on one side of the cheek and then we turn with enough love — I would say cowardice — in us the unsmote cheek to the smiter. You can't do that! It is against the law of nature. America can't do it. When America's cheek is struck by an enemy, she prepares her army to strike back. The Christian government of America can't do it. The Pope of Rome can't do it. If you and I don't wake up to that knowledge and execute the law of an eye for an eye, we might as well be dead and forgotten.

It is better for you and me to just go and commit suicide than for the enemy to come in our homes and drag us down, drag our daughters out, beat, lynch, and rape them while we stand by looking. If you and I are deprived of justice, if the federal government will not punish our murderers and our rapers, I say to you, we must get together and find someway to punish them ourselves!

In the case of a recent lynching in Mississippi, the government agents spent a lot of time trying to find the lynched body to show that he had been lynched. It would have been easier to find the murderers than the dead body. According to the papers — that is all you and I have to go by — the government knows the lynchers. But since finding the lynchers — according to the papers — they have turned the lynchers over to the judges of their own native state and court then they will be freed. As all the other lynchers of our people have been freed.

We have come to the point where we must find justice for ourselves or commit suicide. What good is your life and my life if we have no protection? If I were a Black woman, and my men were such cowards that they would not try and defend me and the children I had produced, I would get a shotgun and kill myself. This is nothing but right. This thing has come to a point of explosion. I am your brother. Your hurt is my hurt. It doesn't make any difference with me what religion you are as long as you are a Black man or a member of the darker people. You and I are brothers. Your hurt is my hurt. How many years have you been frightened? "Keep your mouth shut. Don't say that. It is not time." When is it going to get time for you to speak up for yourselves? You can't blame the government for not giving you anything when you are not asking for anything. The only thing that you are pleading for is a job. Is it not true that John Hawkins, the slave trader of our people, brought you and me here for just the purpose of working for the white man? He didn't bring you here to make you the white man's equal. It is certainly evident by now that it was never intended that you be a full citizen, owner or a significant office holder in America. Your role was that of a slave. Today, even though four hundred years have elapsed, that intent underlies your role in the American body politic.

How pathetic a sight many of us make as we boast of our meager education and the attainment of a measure of economic growth! All these things are an illusion. When rightly viewed, your education has been designed by your oppressors with the specific intent of keeping you in servitude. Your economic growth has been achieved by installment buying which is now clearly shown to be a Bangor's rope about the neck of the Black man. Our oppressors own and control everything. We have nothing. What, then, is the basis of our vaunted and foolish pride? Something must be wrong upstairs.

I ask you how in the name of common sense can we be satisfied with our roles of servitude and as the helpless victims of injustice? If we have simple intelligence and love for our fellowmen we must sound the alarm and let the world know we are not satisfied. We must shake off the dead, dumb and blind shackles that have beset us for generations and move toward unity of our kind. This is the truth. The truth hurts. I will speak it or die. I am not afraid to die for truth indeed. I did not take this mission to try and save my life. I took the mission to fulfill truth even at the cost of death.

We must unite at all costs. Once united, we must stand fully packed as a wall against injustice. If your brother does not want to unite with you, then you must teach him, cajole him, urge him, and persuade him by all methods available until he realizes that he, too, must give his all on the altar of justice. For what if ten million of us die in the process, the remaining seven million or more of us will enjoy freedom, justice and equality!

Allah is sufficient for all our needs. This is why I do not have to beg from our oppressors or march on their Capitol with my hat in my hand. For how can I on one hand preach the doom of the oppressive system and then with the other hand ask alms of the oppressor. Allah is our God. We are His Blessed. He has given all the world to us if we would but first give our all to Him. I met with Allah as Moses met with Jehovah. Allah has revealed the truth unto me. It is up to you to believe it or let it alone. But this does not negate the fact that I know the end of it all. I know tomorrow. I would be happy to tell it to you if you will believe it.

I want you to know that our oppressors are exerting every effort to prevent you and me from uniting. They do not want a united Negro, they do not want an Islamic so-called Negro. They know that Islam frees Black men from fear. As a result, it sets the oppressor's teeth on edge. The power of Islam in best seen when compared to the failure of Christianity:

First, Christianity has failed you because it was the religion which first placed you in slavery.

Secondly, Christianity has failed you because through its doctrine of turning the other cheek it has rendered you incapable of defending yourself in the hour of peril.

Thirdly, Christianity has failed you because it has caused you to forsake the pursuit of justice in this world in the pursuit of an illusory and nonexistent justice beyond the grave.

Now, my beloved, you are faced with the same problem that beset Moses and the children of Israel during the era of the Egyptian captivity.

Pharaoh did not want Moses to preach the religon of Jehovah in Egypt because Pharaoh knew such preaching would bring damnation to his wicked kingdom. So it is that your oppressors did not want you to hear the gospel of the Black man. They know that this gospel will one day be their undoing.

Pharaoh did not want Moses to call the Jews to the wall to wail at sundown. He knew that once the Jews were united in the name of the religion of their fathers they would no longer abide in slavery with a docile air.

Pharaoh did not want Moses to teach the gospel of justice on this side of the grave. He knew that once the Jews determined in their hearts to seek justice here and now they would rise up and demand a place in the sun.

So, then, it is with us. Our oppressors are determined to keep our eyes in the sky while they control the land under our feet. They are determined to bog us down in an impractical ethic of turning the other cheek the better that they may smite our cheeks and rob our pockets.

We must not be deceived by the rush toward integration that has become the theme of the past few years. Just as the Romans were to beware of slavemasters bearing integration. Why, I ask you, after four hundred years of murder, rape and slavery, do our oppressors now come waving the olive branch of integration? Is it that they really love us; is it that they are sincerely sorry for their sins and seek restitution? If they love us, then why was there no evidence of this love in the hearts of their forefathers when they sold our forefathers like cattle on the auction block? If they are really seeking to atone, then why do they not offer us some measure of restitution — an area of this country we can call our own—to the sons and daughters of the embattled?

They are not come to this hour because they love us nor is integration a sign that they are sorry for their sins. The blunt fact is, our oppressors see fire coming. They see the handwriting on the wall and know what it means. They would have you believe that the days ahead hold glory for the Christian world.

My beloved, I, Elijah Muhammad, who must speak if it kills me and who will die rather than lie, tell you this: I know tomorrow! I know the end of it all! Tomorrow is not heaven for the Christian world! Tomorrow is hell for the Christian world!

You have a blind spot because you have not come to the religion of your people. Instead you are weeping and moaning over the death of Jesus two thousand years ago. You are going insane over the preaching of Jesus' life and death. Yet, you don't weep, moan and go insane over the rapes and lynching of your own people in your own time. It is a modern disgrace to see you shouting and having spasms in church over the mistaken notion that God gave His only son to save the Christian world. What a shame!

What fool God would give His only son to save the devil?

What fool people will give their all in the vain hope that the devil can change his horns and lay down his pitchfork?

The religion that has brought us to the brink of destruction is the way of our oppressors. It is not our faith. It is not natural to us. Even more our oppressor cannot follow the very religion he would teach us. I have no alternative but to tell you that there is no life

14

beyond the grave! There is no justice in the sweet bye and bye! Immortality is now, here! We are the blessed of God! We must exert every means to protect ourselves!

The message I bring is not for the cowards. Those of you who follow me must be ready to withstand the barbs and insults of those who come to investigate, pry, and claim that our ultimate aim is to undermine the American way of life. We have no such intentions. Our critics know it. There is nothing under the rug or subversive about what I say and teach. It is shouted over the air, in the newspapers, on the street corners. Why, then should you be intimidated by those who seek only to throw fear in your hearts and know what we say is right.

How ironic it is that the very people who charge us with disturbing the status quo themselves go around raping, lynching, denying citizens the right to vote and taking to the halls of Congress to call you and me everything from a beast to an amoral entity!

Yet they unite with their own kind. They give aid and comfort to their own kind. They bring their common enemy to naught. When then is it so wrong and subversive that you and I unite for the same end?

If you listen well, you can hear the screams of a Negro - co-ed in Tallahassee as she vainly begs her four white abductors to leave her virtue intact. If you listen a little longer, you can hear the pleas of a Milwaukee Black mother as she begs police to free her six and seven year old daughters from a white abductor who held them captive and took carnal liberties with them for over an hour.

These acts of carnage must come to an end. To that

Some of the devil's disciples are called "father," after the pope, the chief father of Satan's religion, Christianity. The pope claims in the Bible, 'that he will sit in the sides of the north and be like the Most High.' Isa. 14:13,14. And yet Allah (God) promised to pull him down to hell (Isa. 14:15). And Allah is going to pull him down real fast.

The Vatican, the home of the pope, has gotten one of the worst beatings with plagues, snow, ice, and enemies—the worst beatings that you ever could have imagined coming to the head of the church.

This shows that Allah (God), the Supreme Being, does not respect Rome and its father whom they call pope. The Vatican, if it were a holy place, we would not expect to suffer the curse of nature.

We who live in America live in a cursed country. America is a cursed country. America is a divine place of exile for Allah's enemies and he promises to use America now for a lake of fire in which to burn all of his enemies.

The Indians, the first people who were sent—who migrated to America—the Indians were also the enemies of Allah.

Self-first—The "reverends" are the enemies of their (our) own Black People. If the preachers do as the white slave-master tells them to do the white slave-master kills them as he did Rev. Martin Luther King, Jr.

But since they are the devil's disciples, he should kill them if they do not obey him. That is right, if the devil wants to be a god like Allah, for Allah will kill those who do not obey him!

So the devil kills those whom he sent and who will

not obey him—so look out "reverend!" Be careful "reverend!" The white slave-master has proved in our own eyes and hearing by killing Rev. Martin Luther King, Jr. who thought he was blessed to go to heaven; but instead he went to hell with his enemies.

I do not mean a hell that is in the earth someplace, brother. Rev. Martin Luther King, Jr. went to hell in the wickedness of his white enemies—trying to satisfy his white enemies. He gets no credit for all of the work that he did for his enemies, and his enemies know that.

I dare any one of the Christian theologists to try to prove that Rev. Martin Luther King, Jr. went anywhere else. Good man that he was, Rev. Martin Luther King, Jr. was deceived and frightened to his very heart by the enemy.

Self first. Think for self first!! When Rev. Martin Luther King, Jr. talked with me at my home, I saw in him that he wanted to believe me; but, he was so afraid of his enemies.

Self-first, you cannot serve two masters. I tried my best to put fearlessness in him. Rev. Martin Luther King, Jr. admitted to me that I am teaching right. He admitted that the white man is the devil, but he was afraid to take a stand and preach that the white man is the devil.

The white man had set Rev. Martin Luther King, Jr. up with a $50,000 Nobel Peace Prize. For this money the white man desired that Rev. Martin Luther King, Jr. go to hell with the devil. The devil did take Rev. Martin Luther King, Jr. to hell.

If Rev. Martin Luther King, Jr. had lasted to this day, he would have been in the same corner with me.

The devil had Rev. Martin Luther King, Jr. in his power through fear.

But good hearted Black Brother, Rev. Martin Luther King, Jr. had a good heart but he was yet dead spiritually; yet he was smart enough in his studies to see the truth of what I am saying.

So I went down to the Coliseum that we had rented for a mass-meeting and I told the public what a great time Rev. Martin Luther King, Jr. and I had at my home. I told the public what a great man Rev. Martin Luther King, Jr. was, and the white enemy showed Rev. Martin Luther King, Jr. what a great man he (Archdeceiver) was and he set Rev. Martin Luther King, Jr. up with the prize money.

Just as it is written the arch-deceiver is capable of deceiving the whole world, except God's last Messenger (Lamb) (Bible Revelations).

Self-first. Let us try and be ourselves first and stop trying to be like the devil. Black man, you are created Black. You, Black man, are the first and the last. Black man stop trying to be white.

If you see what Allah (God) has prepared for the white slave-master, the devil, you will run from the devil when you get a taste of it. Allah (God) has prepared the fire of hell for them.

The Holy Qur'an teaches that the Black man will wish that between him and the devil was the distance between east and west. But you serve the devil—you love him because he has made you to fear him, from the cradle to the grave.

Wake up and take pride in Black self and come on and follow me. I have the God with me — the God who says that there is no fear for the one who believes in him. Nor shall you grieve.

Just think of the blessing that is in those two promises — no fear — no grief. I know we have feared and grieved much. So if anybody needs a God to remove fear and grief from him, we are certainly the people.

Fear of the devil, the white man, is what keeps us back from enjoying heaven. If we do think to please the devil, we are most certainly members of hell.

Day and night they are killing you and each other, of their kind and yet you want to please the devil. You cannot go to heaven pleasing the devil.

To go to heaven, you have to please God. You, Black man, are directly from the God of heaven. Black man you are created to serve Allah. You were not created to serve the devil.

Come and follow me, and there will be no fear for you, nor shall you grieve. We the Muslims fear none but Allah. If anybody needs the fear removed from him, it is the frightened to death Black man in America.

Self first.

CHAPTER 4

The Black Man

The Black man, for the first time since he has been in the Western Hemisphere, is accepting himself as a Black man and not as a colored man.

Although the Black man has been colored—now the Black man has learned that the coloring was false and that the coloring came from a robber (the devil).

After he (the devil himself) had put our Black fathers asleep to the knowledge of their Black selves, the white man pretty nearly destroyed all of the original color of us; and he has added in his own color.

Never have we, the Black man, been so happy to be called Black. And the Book (Bible) teaches us that God will come one day and God will choose us, the Black people, to be His people.

We did not know anything about the false color part that God had in mind to remove from us; but now God is here among us; and He is teaching us the knowledge of our color; and we love our own Black color.

And now we have learned that the color of our enemy has almost destroyed our original Black; we are now waking up to the knowledge that Black is the first color and the last color, (if there be a last).

And now that we have learned that Black is a better color, we want to be Black. You just do not have a better color than Black. Black looks good all of the time. The beautiful part of Black is that we love Black.

Since we now have the knowledge of the two colors (Black and the false color), we are separating the original Black color from the false color so that we can preserve our own Black color forever.

The knowledge of Black self,given to us by Him Who knows us—we all should be happy and rejoicing to know that we, the Black people were never a wicked people until we followed the wicked - one (the white man) after his wickedness.

God has declared us, the Black man, to be the righteous and God makes it plain to see why we are the righteous. We are from the righteous Black people by nature. We, the Black man, are righteous by creation, and we cannot be other than righteous.

This is the happiest time of our, the Black man's life! It is the happiest time of our life to learn who we are and to learn that who we are, the Black man, is the best of the people!

CHAPTER 5

Under The Shadow of Death

We, the Black lost-found of our people here in America live under the shadow of death by way of cowardly enemies. Every one of us—the cowardly enemies seek our deaths, one way or another.

The cowardly enemies will not fight you as a brave man would fight you if they think that you would fight back. They will steal on you when you least expect an attack from them.

We live under the shadow of death. We fled from the cowardly enemy devils of the South, seeking refuge in the same cowardly enemies' brother in the North. The enemy devils of the South followed us to the North to see that his brother of the North does not treat us any better than they did in the South.

They seek police jobs so that they can beat and kill us who are trying to escape. They seek to kill us, or get us killed, at any price. They do not care about our loyalty to them. In their hearts there is death for us, the Black Man in America.

Today, they hold out promises to you only to deceive you. They know that Allah (God) is here offering to seat us in heaven at once. And since hell is their appointed place, they are trying to get us to go to hell with them on false promises.

I have told you. Believe it or let it alone. We live "Under The Shadow of Death."

CHAPTER 6

Babies Murdered

Today you read and hear that white America is agreeing to kill unborn babies. They have set up a law for it. This is the worse sin that you could agree on — to have your baby killed before its birth. What are you going to do that for?

He tried to put out an old unfounded story that you are getting to be too many people and "We have to cut the birth-rate." Who needs to cut the birth rate? The Black people have no need to cut down; they need to increase the birth rate. The earth and the heavens around the earth are ours.

Who is going to go hungry? Do you not read the past histories of how the righteous were always the winners and the victorious people? So will we be, the winners and the victorious people.

We are not thinking of anyone making us hungry unless it is Allah (God), and He came to feed us as it is written, "My righteous servant shall eat, but ye shall go hungry." And, America, hunger is staring at you now—unemployment—you cannot buy the food that you used to buy, for you have nothing to buy it with.

This is why I plead with you to come join up with me and let us go to the earth and grow our food not go walking around the city with a basket for the devil to drop food into—he will not help you for he will not have any food to drop into his own basket. He has not only food stored up, but he has clothes stored up. He has plenty of this, but that does not mean that he cannot come to hunger and nakedness if Allah (God) strikes at him. Allah (God) brings the wicked into

desolation before they can get started to strike back.

Murder the Black babies? — The only ones he should be thinning out is himself. The earth belongs to the Black People. What do we look like cutting down on our birth - rate. Is there any narrowing of the earth for Us? The earth is being expanded for us. There is plenty of earth for us, for Allah (God) will clear the earth of its wicked population. All of those places will be taken by the Muslims.

My God! To pay attention to the white man and let him slaughter the babies before, and after, their birth—this would be like what the fire-worshippers did, who worshipped the fire-god Moloch. They took their babies and threw them into the fire to be burned up, to show their sincerity to the god of fire.

And, are you going to the enemy of the Black Man to have him deprive you of giving birth to a Black baby, to let him kill it in your worship of him? Do not you think that you are acting like a mighty big fool? I think that you are.

This is our earth. Have they squeezed it up so that there is no place to live, except they kill off the Black people? No. Black brothers and Black sisters, I hope that you will read this and understand that we, the Black people, are the true owners and Allah (God) is giving our earth back to us.

This is what he means as well as the spiritual religion of us, when He Says, "Accept your own." This is our earth. He is telling you to accept it. He will give it to you.

The Bible teaches that "The meek shall inherit the

earth" — the humble, poor people - they will get the earth, for it belongs to them.

We have parables in the Bible which the writers of the history of Jesus tell us were spoken by Jesus—the Parable of the Lost Sheep and the Prodigal Son — they returned and became the owners. This only means you and me. Why do not we take our place?

Why should we give our babies to the enemy to be destroyed because he says you have nothing to feed them with? Follow me and I will show you; you will get more houses than you need and more money than you can spend. Help me, brothers, and Allah (God) will not deprive you of your good reward. I know you understand. What we do for Allah (God) He will do it for us. In this day and time we are all tried— the wicked and the righteous are both tried.

What sin has the poor Black baby done for you to murder it in your womb? He has done nothing. It will come back to you in a terrifying way. Your conscience will condemn you for doing such. All of our evil will come before us in a palpitating form.

Let us not be such fools as to think that we have to cast our babies into the arms of a murderer to murder them for the excuse that he needs to do so in order to feed and house you. No place is crowded but the cities. There is plenty of room in the country.

The Black man has never had a problem. Look at China and India. They do not destroy their babies just because they do not have money. They try to have means to take care of them. China takes care of her population. India does not take care of hers because she depends on Britain and other white people.

We must remember that the white race has no part — no share in our earth. They only had time to live on our earth. They did not have a share of actual earth itself.

So let us not kill our Black people for just the asking of a murderer who was made to murder us. I warn you. Do not think hard of him for doing what he was made for. But I do fault you for following him in what he was made for.

CHAPTER 7

When Abe Lincoln, J.F. Kennedy Spoke Out for Negroes

From the death of Abraham Lincoln to the assassination of President Kennedy, it proves that on each one of these occasions where outlaws over - ruled legal authority, it was in the case of Presidents who opened their mouths and said something favorable for the so - called Negro.

I am not saying that this was the reason President Kennedy was assassinated, but it seems very strange that every President who says something favorable for the so called Negro pays for it with his life.

We also can substantiate this by the fact that any Negro who wants to lead the so - called Negro to a better life and towards true peace, freedom, justice and equality — which he is entitled to enjoy — is also subjected to the same kind of assassinations or attempts at assassination.

I know these to be facts. There are some who seem not to want a true freedom and who will also speak unfavorably and plan unfavorable actions against those who dare to lead a true struggle for justice and equality.

The tragic death of President Kennedy should serve as a warning to all rulers and people of value that values cannot be trusted openly in the presence of thieves and robbers.

There has never been a president elected to such a high office who had the heart of everyone for him, and never was there a king who had the people wholeheartedly with him, regardless of how good the

king, the president, prime minister or the spokesman for the king or president.

There may be some people who do not like the high official holding the top office of the nation. I think that they should be well protected, and all precautionary steps should be taken to insure such persons safety. Riding in open cars or walking openly in the public is usually a needless risk taken by anyone holding such high office, especially when they are political officials.

Those spiritual teachers, such as prophets of God and messengers—their lives have not been spared in the public according to recorded history of the lives of these characters. There are both friends and enemies of public servants and we must be aware of them.

Such outlaw action permitted in America is a disgrace and shame to the government and to people who are recognized as world leaders and examples of what others should do in the way of friendship and co - operation.

With the great scientific advancement that America has made, it does not seem possible in this modern time that the tragedy that took place on the 22nd of November should have happened. This is a long way from the assassination of President William McKinley.

There are sixty-two years between the two assassinations of the Presidents of the United States of America, and with such great advancement in the science of protection, these things should have never happened.

Again, it shows to the world that the government of America and its people are actually given to such outlaw and violent action.

To take human lives at will, disregarding their own legal law against such action, makes the country be classified as a country or government of outlaws—where people have no safety of their lives under the law which claims to safeguard the lives of human beings.

CHAPTER 8

The National Election

The Black man of America has been privileged by the slavemasters' children for the last century to vote for whites for the offices to judge and rule. This freedom to vote has made the Black man in America feel very dignified and proud of himself. He goes to the polls very happy to vote for a white ruler. Today, he is gradually changing to a desire to vote for his own kind for such offices of authority.

We must remember that our vote is strong and powerful only when and where the white man can use it to get in the office over his white opponent. After the election and the victory there are very few favors that come from his office to the Black voters who helped and aided him in getting in the office. Why? Because he does not owe the Black voter anything as long as he has to feed, clothe, and shelter him.

The Black vote could be cast or not cast. The white citizens of the government are going to win and continue to rule anyway.

There is much talk of this man and that man (who shall the vote of the people put in the White House for the next four years?)

How much good have the two parties (Republican and Democrat) done for us for the last century in the way of freedom, justice, and equality? Regardless of what party wins, the die is always set against us (the Black people in America).

Injustice, crooked politics, and the breeding of corruption under crooked politics have been practiced ever since Adam to the present day rulers. Adam was the first crook.

There has not been justice for the Black man in this race of people, and this is why the race suffers from the effect of chaos today.

There are Black politicians who would like to use their Black people for selfish greed and will throw them behind any crook with money. Black politicians of this type have sold their Black brothers to suffering and shame for self elevation with the crook.

This election is one of the most serious in the history of American government, because either party that seeks the office of presidency is faced with the problem of saving the lives of the people of America. If the present party (Democratic) remains in office, you know the answer. If the Republican party takes over, you should know the answer. There will be a lull before the storm. The storm can be delayed and every hour and day that it can be delayed is to your benefit.

The Black man should be very serious and careful about his voting because 90 per cent of the Black votes cast are cast by ones who do not have the knowledge of what they are casting their vote for.

I still say, as I have said for many years, vote for Allah (God) to be your ruler and come follow me.

CHAPTER 9

The Dead are Rising!
They Seek Their Own!

The dead are we, the Black once-slaves of the white man of America. We are a mentally Dead people. We are dead to the knowledge of self and others.

The knowledge of self has now come to us from God, Who Came in the Person of Master Fard Muhammad, to Whom Praises are Due forever!

Master Fard Muhammad, to Whom Praises are Due forever, is A Man. His Teachings bring us into Reality, and not into some kind of spooky, or spirit, or ghost-like teaching.

Master Fard Muhammad, to Whom Praises are Due forever is The All - Wise and Living - God. He Desires that we see Him as He is — a Human Being and not something beyond the family of human beings — spookisms.

We could never ask a formless spirit to lead us because we are not a formless spirit ourselves. Man can only listen to man. Man cannot listen to other than man.

And I have proof—we just never were able to obey anything but ourselves!

We, the once-Dead, mentally, are coming to the knowledge of life;—when we learn this lesson of the living, it will destroy the belief in other than ourself.

Bringing us up in slavery time — putting us to a mental - death was something that the slavemaster and his children did because of their desire to make us into something that was other than the truth in order to be able to keep our minds enslaved!

From the Visit of God, in the Person of Master Fard Muhammad to Whom Praises are Due forever, the Time, now, has come to us, as it is written. That on the Day of Judgment, we will see God as He Is. (Bible, Rev. 1:7.).

The Rise Of The Dead, does not, by any means, mean what you and I were taught when we were little boys and little girls — And even while we are little boys and little girls in man and woman - age, we are still pushed on a babyside, for understanding of the truth.

We, the Black People, are no longer babies — We are babies to no one, except, God Himself! You are fast learning that you are not babies any more but on your Rise Up From The Dead knowledge of Black self, and others.

You are learning fast that Allah (God) Is Fast creating in us a new way of thinking, for the way in which we had been thinking was in a way of untruth and an unseemly way of understanding.

America is a country where evil is dominant and the people in America think nothing but evil! It is very seldom that you can talk to a person without getting the thought, quickly, that their mind is filled with evil!

We, the Black People in America, are called the Dead, spiritually. And, We, the Black People in America, now desire to make for ourselves something better than what the slave - master's children have made of us. We want to make something better of ourselves than what the slave - master's children still do make of us.

Look at the many people who used to be stage -

actors, and who are now forsaking the stage as being a mockery to them and are now former stage-actors who want to be seen and conversed with as civilized Black People; and not as some kind of a stage-actor.

The white stage actors are with some sense because they are civilized. A meaningless act is not enjoyed by a people who are intelligently learned into the knowledge of civilization.

But the poor Black Man in America has no knowledge of any civilization. But the white man has gotten into all of the civilized people of the earth and he knows them and they know him.

This is why now a war between civilizations must take place; because the present ruler (white race) has deceived the whole entire civilized world with their civilization of deceit!

The white race was made for the purpose of making mischief. The white race was made for the purpose of deceit. And, now that Almighty God Has Come to Make Manifest that which has been hidden of the truth, this runs the white man from under his deceitful blanket which had the white man covered.

As the Bible teaches us "God will pull the covering off of the covered and show the nations his (white race's) shame" (Nah. 3:5).

If the white man had not been uncovered by Almighty God Allah Who Came in the Person of Master Fard Muhammad, to Whom Praises are Due forever, — I do not see any cover left for the white man's skin!

By Allah (God) Pulling the cover off of the white race this makes it possible for us, the Black People, who were Dead to the knowledge of the truth, to See

40

the natural characteristics of this deadly white enemy of the Black Man.

Now we can shun our enemy like we do a rattle - snake! When we see the rattle - snake, or hear his rattler sing, we begin to try and seek cover from the rattle - snake if we are not able to kill for we know his deadly sting.

But this snake (white race) has overtaken us and he has bitten us so many times that we have become so poisoned from his poison getting into our blood, from his sting, that it has taken God, now, to Come to Prevent the snake from continuing to sting us.

And Allah (God) has the Cure for our being bitten by the snake. He will Separate both of us from being involved with each other so the snake's poisonous sting will not affect us.

The Black Man in America has never known anyone but the white race; therefore, the Black Man seeks pacification and mercy from a merciless people.

You cannot blame the white man for what he is, you cannot blame him for being merciless, for the white people were made the people that they are.

And the white man has made us, the Black Man, other than our own self. At the present time, we are not like we were when we were created in the Beginning! In the Beginning we were created right—Then, we were deceived by the deceiver who was made a deceiver, by nature.

Our Black People are Rising Up. And we are happy to Rise into the knowledge of self and others. The Rise Of The Dead will be like the blast of a trumpet pretty soon!

The Black People will become into the knowledge of

themselves so fast that it will look like The Rise Of The Dead has taken place at once!

I just love to look at my Black People now. All of them are Rising. And listening to them talk you see how much different they are!

My Black People must get out of the white man's name. But my Black People must be qualified to enter their real Original Name of Almighty God Allah!

Come to the Temple of Islam and learn all about yourself, and after learning all about yourself, you will be able to take those who enslaved you, and wrap them around your little finger and you will not feel them on your little finger until you see them on your little finger and shake them off!

Allah (God) Loves you and I love you.

We want to Build Up this world for ourselves, to live in this world in Peace and happiness!

CHAPTER 10

Resurrection of Our People

The old world must be removed to make way for the new world. There is a universal struggle being waged by the old world against the beginning of the new world. Will the old world's opposition prevent the establishment of the new world? According to recorded history, the efforts being made by the old world against the beginning of a new world will fail as did former opponents of Allah.

According to the history of Noah, the people ridiculed the very thought of Allah bringing a flood to drown them. Noah was laughed at and scorned for preaching such a doctrine. According to the Bible and Holy Qur'an, he was called a liar and looked upon as a crazy person. Some of the members of Noah's family joined the mockers and disbelievers of Allah and His Messenger, who was Noah. They met the same fate as the others who disbelieved.

The opposition of that world to the advent of a better world was a total failure. So shall it be with those today who oppose the beginning of a new world of righteousness (Islam.) In the time of Abraham and his nephew (Lot)—before the birth of Ishmael and Isaac, Abraham's two sons—the people, mockers and haters of truth and righteousness in that part of the world (the cities of Sodom and Gomorrah,) had become victimized to every imaginable evil. They even threatened the life of the preacher of righteousness, Lot, disregarding the strangers (angels) visiting Lot—until it was too late. So it is with the opponents of the Messenger of Allah today in America.

The wicked always believe they are mightier than Allah, and they make a supreme effort to thwart the plan and purpose of Allah to bring about a better world. They always love to attack the Messenger to try to condemn him as a liar. Trying to prove the Messenger a liar means calling Allah a liar. The Holy Qur'an repeatedly prophesies a miserable, shameful, and disgraceful defeat for the disbelievers and hypocrites in their campaign against the last Messenger of Allah, whom Allah would raise in the time of the resurrection of the dead people.

Messengers are never sent; they always are raised in the midst of those whom Allah would warn so they can't claim that they did not understand the language of the Messenger, or say that he was a foreigner or stranger. The Messenger is one from them.

For nearly thirty-four years, I have served you, just as Allah's warners-of-old served a hard-hearted and hard-headed, disbelieving people, who were great lovers of the enemies of Allah and the true religion, Islam (which means entire submission to Allah's will.) There is mockery, and evil plans are made against my life by the wicked—just as they were made against Noah and subsequent prophets.

The powerful, rich world of Christianity — especially America—is made to seem as immovable as the mountains. But it is not impossible to remove mountains; they can be removed by high explosives. So wealth and power also can be reduced to nothing.

We are now living in the judgment, or doom, of the white man's world. Preparations have been made to meet every effort by the white man to oppose the beginning and setting up of Allah's new world of righteousness (Islam.) The government (U.S.A.) today watches my followers with an evil eye, seeking to deceive anyone who would enter the fold to help further the cause of truth and the upliftment of the mourning heads and the grieving hearts of the American so-called Negroes; to help make them a nation of righteousness and justice to serve as a star for the nations of their own kind forever. The U.S. government is active in its deceitful work of trying to slow the progress of the resurrection of our people.

American whites want us to reject Allah and the true religion, Islam, and believe in their false religion and false god, whom they cannot make manifest to you. They cannot prove to you, in this day and time, that Christianity is a defense for you—as well as for themselves— against their doom.

America must be taken and destroyed, according to the prophets, at the time and end of the wicked world, where the lost-and-found members of the ancient and aboriginal people are found. America hates and mistreats her slaves to the extent that it has reached the heart of Allah and the righteous people of the earth (the Nation of Islam.)

We read where our Black brothers refer to the American so-called Negroes as their brothers, while according to the preachings of some of these lost-and-found members of the aboriginal nation of the earth, they would rather have themselves referred to as the brothers of their enemies.

The extent to which the enemy has poisoned the minds and hearts of my people here in America is shameful. They willfully do anything to deceive the so-called Negroes into going to their doom with them. There is no way for the enemy of Allah, His Messenger and His people (the darker people of the earth) to find strength, power and wisdom enough to win in a war against Allah. As it is written in the Christian Bible and many other places:

"But the day of the Lord will come as a thief in the night; in thee, which the heavens shall pass away with a great noise, and the elements shall melt with fervent heat, the earth also and the works that are therein shall be burnt up." (Bible, Peter, 3:10.)

The earth shall not be burned, it will be here for many thousands of years to come. Only that on the earth (the devils) which has sinned against Allah and His laws will be destroyed. The earth, the sun, the moon, and the stars have never disobeyed Allah since their creation.

CHAPTER 11

Opposers of Truth

Adam and Eve (the father and mother of the white race—(Yakub is the real name) refused the religion of Islam (peace) because of the nature in which they were made. This makes it impossible for the white race to submit to Allah and obey His law of righteousness. This, the lost-found members of the Asiatic nation from the Tribe of Shabazz must learn of the white race: that it is a waste of time to seek mercy and justice from a people who by nature do not have it for each other. They talk and preach the goodness of God and His prophets only to deceive you, who by nature are of the God of Righteousness, into following them away from our God to a god who does not exist.

Our future is at stake, and 99 per cent of us do not know it. With ever-evil snoopers around you seeking an excuse to do their worst to you makes it hard for the 99 per cent ignorant to ever know the truth. Their greatest desire is to prevent you from ever accepting the truth. They claim the truth to be subversive and hate teachings. They seek any kind of charge to place against us to get revenge for our preaching the truth. They tap our telephones, eavesdrop and follow us around from place to place, and use tape recording machines; and the hypocrites and stool pigeons among us keep them up to date on what we say and do. They are bold enough to even ask your own relatives to help them to do you evil; and due to fear and ignorance on the part of my poor people, the enemies hire them to destroy themselves. Truth hurts the guilty. Will persecuting and murdering the truth bearer help the evil doers in this late hour of the day (the end of their time)?

Our problem must be solved, saith Allah, the God of Righteousness, Who is with you and me to raise us up, the poor lost and found members of the Original Owners of the Planet Earth (the tribe of Shabazz). A good solution is as follows:

Stop opposing the spread of Islam (peace) among us. Let us go back to our God, Allah, and our religion of Islam (peace). Since you will not give us (the so-called Negroes) equal justice, and do not want social mixing with your free slaves because of degrading and lowering your own status in the eyes of the world, help us to go for ourselves, either out or in your country.

For 400 years, we have served you with our labor, sweat and blood, the lash of your whip, your killings, lynching and burning of our innocent Black flesh, without even a hearing in a court of justice, nor even our murderers being punished. Although we are marched before your enemies, and there we pour out our lives for the freedom of your lives, children and your country, we return home to meet an even worse enemy. We are hated and kicked out in certain places like an "unwanted dog" who has caught the game but was not given a taste of it (only that which the hunter could not and should not eat himself). The dog, being too ignorant to recognize the injustice done to him by his master, will jump to his feet again at the call of his master to offer his life for his master's life. This we have and still are doing for you.

We are not wanted in your better neighborhoods. In

many places we have to be guarded and protected by your armed forces in order to live in a house which one of your kind has sold to us. Yet, we are the most peaceful and humblest of the population. We are taxed equally and perhaps more than those of our own kind who are the real citizens and owners of this country, America, though our labor and the labor of our fathers made and built it for you.

Think it over—millions of us working, fighting and dying at your hand and others for four hundred years without a home which we can call our own—not being allowed to worship our God, religion, nor have unity among self and our kind without being charged with the worst of crimes: subversiveness, sedition, treason and seeking to overthrow the government by force (though we have no arms to do such) just to have an excuse for your persecuting and seeking to kill the same poor four hundred year old slave.

CHAPTER 12

Deceivers and The Deceived

We,the whole nation of the lost-found members of the Black nation in America, must remember that for the past four hundred years we have been reared by the enemies of our fathers.

According to their own history writing,bringing us from our native land and people into the Western Hemisphere was not for the purpose of making themselves friendly people to us and our nation, but to deceive us as being that which they actually were not- a friend and advisor to us, while at the same time, depriving us of truth, justice and equality even now, after four hundred years of servitude slavery.

We must remember that the deceiver actually has deceived us. The coming of God in the Person of Master Fard Muhammad(to Whom praise is due forever) is to make manifest this arch deceiver's work against us and to acquaint us with the nature of the arch deceiver—that deceit is part of his very nature.

He (Allah)comes to give us the knowledge of the god of evil who had freedom for the past six thousand years to deceive not only you and me but also the entire nations of the earth.

This is the greatest salvation that God (Allah) could bring to you and me — to know the source of our trouble and its cause. The power of the Manifestor is to remove this cause which has affected the Black nation for six thousand years.

It is worth the heaven and the earth to us when we agree on not trying to make them our friends, which by nature they cannot be, even if they wanted to. Only a few have the belief of goodness. By nature, they are not good, but they can practice goodness.

Our predicament and position makes us the victim of deceit of these great scientific deceivers, the white race. They put us to sleep as babies, and they know the type of noise that will awaken the sleeping baby. The noise is that which Allah (in the Person of Master Fard Muhammad) has made. And He (Allah) has missioned me to continue to make that noise until all of our people are fully awakened from the slumber of the arch deceiver of the nations of the earth.

Surely not all are really working to keep us blind, deaf, and dumb to the knowledge of the deceiver; but the few who would help us endanger their own lives in trying to help us.

As you see, the Christian priest Groppi, in Milwaukee — who professes to be trying to help those who want to live next door and in the house of the children of our father's slave master — is having trouble. Even this easily can be classified as deceitful work against true freedom, justice and equality for our people. This priest Groppi is having trouble among other open vicious haters of you and me, of his kind.

This priest wants to help the poor Black man here in America, and especially in Milwaukee, to accept false friendship; to forever be at their mercy to rule spiritually, economically and politically.

He is not trying to teach the Black men that they should not want to sell themselves back to the slave master for a morsel of pottage. The priest knows by the scripture in his Bible that the time is ripe for the

51

total freedom of the 400-year-old slave of the white man to go to his own (earth). The priest is wise to you, that you should have a place to live wherever you want.

He would not have dared teach this openly before this day and time-the end of this world. The others are so evil and vicious to do us harm that great gangs of white people out in the streets will attack one poor Black man going through the area in his car and will yell "Get the nigger!"

This is a coward's action of the white man in America ever since we have been here — going after the so-called Negro to do him harm. He always wants a hundred whites to attack that one Negro. This shows cowardice and the savage instinct of the white race against Black people. The Black man can put a stop to such attackers of this evil force, but it is not the way of Allah (God.) It is not the way of the prediction, as the priest knows.

The coming of Allah in search for the Black lost members of their nation today is to make Himself known, so He can conquer our captors by using weapons against which they have no power. He (Allah) will bring attacks of divine judgment of their world without the use of contrived weapons.

The weapons of war used by God in the past history of the destruction of the enemies of God — such as Noah's people, Lot's people, and Moses' people-are an example of what he will use today. The weapons are the forces of nature against which we have no defense.

America is under such divine attack now, in storms as rain, hail and earthquakes—(the latter is yet to take place.) A terrific drought is on its way, too, against America. The Book must be fulfilled. The Bible and Holy Qur'an both refer to all that I have said.

This is the divine judgment to bring vicious America to her knees. She (America) hates the people of God and the Negroes do not know that they are really the people of God. This is the great truth that you must come into the knowledge of—that you are a member of the family of God, and not a member of the family of the devil. But you follow the devil, contrary to your own nature. The natural man (Black) is of God Himself.

We have been deceived of righteousness, justice, and equality by the arch deceiver. We have been taken from the knowledge of self as being the true people of God and that God is present seeking us to place us again into the orbit of the Divine Supreme Being where we can rotate in submission to the will of God as the entire universe is doing — except the white race.

We cannot set up a better government for our people by using the corrupt political activities of this people — the arch deceivers. All of their work was based upon deceiving the nation, not to bring them into friendly brotherhood and prosperity for the Black man.

Even today, after a hundred years of so-called freedom, he is still against you going free. This is your trouble today. You are deceived, and deceived by the enemy you think is a friend, but take note of what he offers you. He is offering you only temporary enjoyment — and not a permanent enjoyment for your people. We want some earth, and not a temporary room in the house of our enemy.

Let the political and spiritual leaders unite on such a stand as getting some earth for the people, and not getting just a job and a chance to loll around, sleeping and allowing the enemy to protect our responsibility for self. We must bear our own responsibility.

This the God of justice and truth will force you to do, before He will be defeated. His purpose and aim is to reunite us to our own. He will fight the arch deceiver with the forces of nature and with His own wisdom, which has no equal, to make you and the enemy bow to His will.

This is the judgment of the world and especially of the white man in America, who has been here for 400 years, living between the two oceans — the Atlantic, and the Pacific — to do as he pleases. The slave is deprived of the freedom to do as he pleases, but to do as the slave master pleases.

Our great misunderstanding of self and of others lies in the deceit of the arch deceiver of us. They will never teach you and me to do good for self, only under their own power and dictatorship.

What we need is to unite, not demanding and marching all over the country to live near the white man in his home — but demand a separate place for us in this country and help us with the means of civilization, as he had to get started, limiting the time to get started within the next twenty or twenty-five years.

Many scientists think that it is too late for this demand because of the anger of Allah (God) against America for her evil done to us, but Allah has power over all things and He does that which he wills to do.

It is up to America, if she wants to help us. It would be a great good, putting us on the way to self, by any evil one or nation. The God of justice would grant them a reward for doing such, as no good act goes without its reward.

They deceive the so-called Negro under temptation, filth, indecency and a promise that they will be given jobs and new homes next door to them in the same territory which their very nature is against and which is without any future. It is temporary enjoyment. We want something permanent. Give us a few of these states to live in to ourselves which we have well earned with four hundred years of free labor.

When he sees that his life and your life are at stake to try to accept the present plans, filled with deceit to the Negro, both you and he will welcome an opportunity to agree on the kind of program.

Unite with me, Black America, for your salvation.

CHAPTER 13

Evil Spreading Far, Wide

Never since the creation of Adam and Eve have there been such chaotic times as we are witnessing today— with the worst yet to come! There is no peace among the nations of the earth.

The only few people who enjoy peace of mind and contentment in this day and time are the elect of God, though they are persecuted from city to city and falsely accused and denied the credit due them because of their righteousness in the midst of the wicked who have ruled the world.

By no means can the righteous be represented for their righteous sake by the evil-doers of the world.

"God is despised and rejected; evil is accepted and honored; justice stands afar off, and equity cannot come in," says the prophet Isaiah in the Bible.

The Holy Qur'an warns us to fear a day when evil is spread far and wide in the days of God's presence at the end of the satanic world to bring it to naught.

Allah (God) causes the evil world to be upset since they have been the enemies of peace and the haters and destroyers of the righteous who would have brought them peace if they had accepted those worthy (the Prophets).

But they rejected all; Jesus charged them with being the murderers of the righteous from Abel to Zachariah—we can very well add more, and say from Abel to Muhammad.

Today, America professes to be the most Christianized country on our planet. But actually she is not; for Christian means to be crystallized into one. Spirtually, that One refers to the Christ.

Christ means the "One Who is coming at the end of the world of the wicked as a crusher." His name actually means "One who is annointed to crush the wicked." The real satanic people are the white race who have disguised themselves to deceive the Black people to follow them. They just use the name, Christian, which means to be Christ-like.

They have set up a head for their religion in Rome, Italy, with the pope or father who represents himself as being the intercessor or viceregent; meaning one who is second only to Christ or God and intercedes for the people's sins and recognition of God. But he has no Divine backing.

This false regime should be destroyed by the Christ, the Crusher of the wicked, the Great Mahdi of Islam (Allah 'God' in person).

These are the days of God's or Christ's presence to destroy this evil world with all the deceptions that the people should again labor under a wicked and merciless ruler, the devil. The presence of Allah has upset the devils who have had and exercise total control over the world under falsehood and have made evil to appear fair-seeming.

The so-called Christian world has never before displayed such madness as they do today. Since they cannot hide their real wickedness and deceitful ways, they are angry.

According to the preaching and teaching of Christianity, they prophesy that they alone would be the happy group that would welcome the coming of the Messiah, the Christ, or the Mahdi. But the Bible condemns them; that they were angry and sought to hide their faces from Him (God).

It should be clear to you today that Christian America does not want such preaching as entire submission to the will of Allah (Islam). The Christians hate the very names of God: such as Muhammad, Omar, Karriem, Ali, Hassan, which are attributes of God.

The Jesus prophesied that they would hate you for His (God's) name sake, for having one of His names. Because the names of God are to live forever. No The names of God are to live forever. No other people on earth have the names of God but the Muslims.

So the coming of the Just One makes manifest to you this evil race of sinners. And they will be against His (God's) presence; be angered because of Him and will seek to destroy Him and His messenger as it is prophesied (2nd Psalms).

CHAPTER 14

Every Nation Has A Term

"And Every nation has a term; so when its term comes, they cannot remain behind the least while, nor can they precede (it)."—Holy Qur'an 7:34.

There was a term for the people of Noah, Lot and Moses. This also holds true in the life and death of individuals — all is under the control of Almighty Allah — especially when a divine beginning and ending has been appointed for the accomplishment of a certain work that must be done by the life or the life of peoples.

The above chapter and verse of the Holy Qur'an is a warning to the present nation whose term is now coming to an end. If we know what is said to us and what is written by the prophets for us to read, study and ponder over, and if we understand, we should not fall victims to misunderstanding and disbelief.

The trouble with the Black man in America is that he is heedless of the truth, for he was reared by slave foster-parents who were his enemy (the white race). They caused him to become heedless. It was the intention of the enemy to make the Black man an enemy to the truth as he himself was and is.

This the enemy was successful in doing, for the aboriginal Black man in America is referred to as being blind, deaf, and dumb, and in many instances as dead. This is the work of the enemy.

Therefore, it took one who is our friend and not our enemy, to do good to us and restore us to life (mentally). The children of the fathers (slavemasters) who took our life (mental) are working just as faithfully as their fathers did.

However, since 100 years have elapsed from the time of their slave-fathers, the children are wiser and educated more in methods to keep the aboriginal Black man in America blind, deaf and dumb.

In the days of servitude slavery — of our grandparents — the white slavemaster did not even give them good food. Today, you can buy good food if you have the money. However, much of it is poisoned (by chemicals used). The slavemaster would offer a piece of fried chicken and a biscuit with a little butter on it to a so-called Negro as an inducement for him to teach or preach what the slavemaster wanted him to, to the other slaves on Sunday morning. The slaves did not have the theology of the scriptures and he made his other brothers spiritually blind, deaf and dumb.

The same goes for the preachers of today, as you can see. They preach for a reward from both white and Black. I have tried them for many years. They are as their fathers were. They desire the exaltation of the white man. They want him to give them better positions and they will offer to cut off the heads of their Black brothers if it will please "master."

Although I live in a neighborhood with white neighbors, I do so for the purpose of proving that I can live in their neighborhood just as cleanly and noiselessly as they do. White people do not like you to come into their neighborhood, jumping on them and licking them in the mouth like a puppy.

They do not want their friends to think that they are taking you for an equal. He will talk to you as a friend when he is not in the presence of members of his society. They do not like you coming into the block beating your wife or girl friend and drinking in front of their houses. No decent and intelligent person likes this, whether he is white as snow or Black as the ace of spades.

You can go to the jungle and the pygmy will not want this. Late at night he and a gang of monkeys will come out and beat you up.

The American so-called Negro has been made out of himself and kind by the white Americans. He must now be reformed. In fact, God has promised him a new body. The Bible and the Holy Qur'an teach us that we will be a new people altogether. He was destroyed and acts ignorant and foolish. He is not aware of his ignorant actions because he has become a part of ignorance.

Now the end of the term which was set for the white man has come. The average so-called Negro, the lost found member of the Black nation does not know that this is the end of the world of the white man (his rule over the Black nation). He will not listen to one of his own kind who tells or teaches him of the time and doom of the world that we have known (white man's world).

They offer high positions and money to the so-called Negro intellectual politicians who will work against the good of the Black American people. They will accept such gratuity, for they have been deprived of love for self and kind. What do they care about the millions who are sprawled in the mud of civilization? They are content as long as they eat the buttered biscuit and the fried chicken (as their slave-fathers did).

You would not think that they would hire themselves out to be stool pigeons—white man's boot-lickers and Uncle Toms in these modern times of advanced education—but they are doing just that.

They do not want the praise and exaltation of God and their own Black people. They want it from the slavemasters' children. The slavemasters' children will give it to them as long as they reject themselves and kind and worship and exalt the white people.

The white man is very clever in making a public fool of the Black man. They show the brown, yellow and red man what a good job they have done on the Black man in America and throughout the earth. He is doing what nature bids him to do.

I do not blame the white man anymore for making fools of our people. It is the nature of the white man to make a fool of our people, but it is not the nature of our people to allow him to a make a fool of us.

But, when you have been given the knowledge of yourself, the nature in which God created you, and you still allow the enemy to make a fool of you, then you do not have the sympathy of God and the righteous, not after knowledge.

The divine term that was given to the white race to allow them to make a fool of the Black man and rule him with tricks is now up. The devil with his tricks must be removed.

He was given this chance to deceive you with his tricknology; and therefore, God will not hinder the devil from tricking you if he can. This is written in the Holy Qur'an, Chapter 7. But God promised hell-fire to both the devil and his followers whom he can get from the Black Nation.

Therefore, you and I — after knowledge of the devil, his tricks, and his term — should not blame anyone but ourselves, if we allow the devil to trick us, for that is the job of the devil. It is his nature. We blame ourselves and not the enemy.

You lust for his half-nude women and thirst for whisky and beer. You desire gambling, robbing and killing each other for the personal property of others. This is the work of the devil upon you. You do not have to allow him to cause you to live such a life. Do not blame them, blame your foolish self.

It has always been the policy of the white man to use a Black man against a Black man—especially leaders. Look at history. See how he has deceived and killed off the Black leaders of foreign lands and then they took over themselves. This should be a lesson for you and me.

We, the Muslims, have watched our people who have come among us as eyes and ears (stool pigeons) for white folks. When they have become converted to the truth and join us, they confess that they are ashamed that have worked against us, for the sake of a few perishable dollars.

We know that the white man is our enemy and wherever we are, he offers some silly so-called Negro a higher office and higher pay to work against us Muslims, the righteous, or any so-called Negro. Whether he be a Baptist, Methodist, Holy Roller or sanctified, some lazy so-called Negro will work against him for the white man.

It is a shame in such modern times to see Black politicians and preachers accepting positions to work against their own Black people for a few dollars from a race whose time has come to an end.

We are justified in taking it if the white man gave us a billion or a hundred billion dollars. We deserve it. But we are not justified to sell our lives for such a gift in this day and time.

Declare yourself a Muslim and see how much the devil will give you. He would say, "We will give it to you if you preach that we are not the devil." We would answer, "that is just the same as saying, 'If you do not teach the truth of me, so that I can continue to deceive the world of your kind, I will help you.'"

Remember what the Bible teaches us that Satan said to Jesus, "...All these things will I give thee, if thou wilt fall down and worship me." Matt: 4:9. And he showed him the kingdoms of the world.

Perhaps you will be offered the world of the wicked pretty soon. If so, the Bible says, "What profit a man if he gain the world and lose his own life (soul)?" This is a warning to the preachers.

The little money, with its dying value, will not help you against God's aims and purpose of the resurrection of the dead Lost-Found members of the Aboriginal Nation. You will lose your lives for so doing-and you should, for you cause innocent ones who are blind, deaf and dumb to go to hell with yourself and the enemy.

Allah, (God) came forth in the Person of Master Fard Muhammad, to Whom praise is due forever, the Son of Man, as it is written, seeking to save that which was lost and to restore again that which had gone astray.

He said to me that He would eat rattlesnakes to

64

save our lives and that He would walk forty miles up a mountain to teach just one in order to save his life in exchange for our safety and return to our own.

I have taken Him for my God and my Saviour. I advise you to do the same, regardless of the offers of money, which is fast becoming worthless.

Jesus refused the money and dwelt upon the truth that is written that we must not worship Satan. Satan's place is behind us and not in front of us.

It is the nature of Satan to try and deceive the very angels in heaven; not to think of the fools who are in his hell. In the Bible (Rev.), it is written that you would accept the enemy and go down in a lake of fire with him.

Read the following passages of your Bible which dwells on the time and yourselves: Prov. 14:12, 19:20, 25:8, Isa. 9:7, 46:10, 2:19. Eze. 7:2,3, 21:25, 35:5, Dan. 5:6, 11:45, 1 Pet. 4:7, Rev. 21:6, 22:13.

Holy Qur'an translation by Maulana Muhammad Ali—Chapters 104:1-7, 75:1-15, 35:40, 7:22, 103:2, 4:117-120, 7:20,21.

CHAPTER 15

America

The American white people are more concerned about mistreating the Black once-slave of America than America is concerned with any nation on earth that is attacking her out-lying posts. Her enemies are intensifying their attacks on her. America is right out of the frying pan into the fire all over the earth, due to her evil intentions against her loyal Black once-slaves. Her talk of evil-doing against the Black once-slave in America is worse than it is against independent nations that are trying to attack and destroy her country. White America has more hatred for the Black once-slaves in her midst who are faithfully fighting on the firing- line to help her against her enemy than she is against the enemy that they are shooting down.

White America talks of building concentration camps (prison houses) for the Black once-slave (the Black man in America). I am told that America already has concentration camps built for this purpose. Concentration camps are jail houses — prison houses. This is why I cry day and night to my Black brothers to seek refuge in Allah (God) in such a time as this.

The Muslims do not have to worry about any such imprisonment, for the Muslim is already a citizen of the Nation of Islam, and we have our own people (Muslims) to deliver us by the order of God. This is why it is so necessary that the Black man in America accept Allah (God) and His name and get out of the name of the enemy white slave-master, who does not seek to bring about peace for us; but the enemy seeks to bring about our death.

White America wants her Black once-slave to suffer that which is not due to the Black once-slave. The Black once-slave has not sinned nor has the Black once-slave attacked other nations except under the order of his white slave-master.

CHAPTER 16

Independence Day

Whose independence? Since 1776 you, Black man, have been worshipping the 4th of July along with the real author of the 4th of July...(the white man) as a day of Independence for themselves.

It is the white slave-master and his children who enjoy setting forth the 4th of July as a day of rejoicing over achieving this country's independence from any other foreign source.

Now, the history of the 4th of July shows that it is the Independence Day of the American white man. They wrote the Declaration of Independence for themselves. The white man did not put anything in the Declaration of Independence for the benefit of the Black Man, who was the servitude - slave of the white man, at that time.

The joy which the Black slave experienced on these holidays of the white man was due to the Black man getting rest from his labor and the days which the white man had set aside for celebration. That is all the Black slave was rejoicing over...that he did not have to work that day.

But, you are free now; and you do not need this for an excuse for your worship of the 4th of July. There is no further need for us to worship the gaining of the white man's independence.

Let us take a look again at our own Black independence and how it came on this same day of the 4th of July... at the Coming of Allah (God) Who came in the Person of Master Fard Muhammad, to Whom praises are due forever, on July 4, 1930.

The significance of His coming to us, on the

Independence Day of the white man, is very great. It is their day of great rejoicing. As with former peoples and their governments, their destruction took place when they were at the height of their rejoicing.

Nebuchadnezzar, according to the Bible history of him, (Dan. Ch.4) was walking around in his palace and proudly looking around and admiring the skill of the work he had set up and said, "has not all this my hand wrought?" The Bible teaches us that while the words were in his mouth, the end came. Allah (God) changed his mind and heart from that of a civilized man to the mind and heart of a beast. He had the brain reactions of a wild beast and he was cast out a among the dumb brutes.

What does that signify? It gives us a gleaning into the history of the white man and his being cast out of the society of the Muslims six thousand years ago...after he was made and then started trouble among the people of righteousness.

Trouble-making caused the white man his exile into the hills and cave-sides of West Asia, as Europe was called at that time, so Allah (God) taught me. Its name was changed to Europe after the white man was cast into that area. Europe means a place where people are bound in, to keep them out of the society of the righteous.

Moses made (white man) as independent race, thru the guidance which Allah (God) gave Moses, to guide the white man out of his savage cave life, and put him on the road of conquest of the Black man.

For four hundred years the white man swallowed us, (the Black man of America) up. He did not put us in a hole of the earth but he swallowed us up by keeping anything like wisdom from coming to us. He set a bound against our own Black people visiting us in order to prevent them from teaching us anything other than what the white man was teaching our Black slave-fathers.

This caged us in, and made just as secure a cage as the literal cage of Europe that the Arab people put the white man in six thousand years ago.

The 4th of July is the Day of rejoicing of the white man over his opponents, for the Western Hemisphere. He wrote his Constitution for his own white people...not for his Black slave.

Since this is his day which he set aside for himself, then what part, Black brother, do you have in this day? Your part is not mixed with his part in the way of his own white politics and physical independence.

But, as I called your attention to proud King Nebuchadnezzar's history and what happened to him at the height of his kingdom, Allah (God) never detroyed a powerful people nor deprived them of self - independence when they were in trouble or when they were sick with grief. He made them to feel happy. He made them think that they would live forever.

So it was with the coming of Allah (God) in the Person of Master Fard Muhammad, to Whom praises are due forever, on His coming to us, on the 4th of July, 1930. His presence meant the destruction of the independence of the white race and especially, America...over the Black man.

Allah (God) visited the Black slave, for he is more in need of help to enjoy freedom of self.

Since Allah (God) came for the purpose of bringing self-independence to the Black slave, then His going forth is with justice (Bible Rev: 19-11th.)

To show Allah's (God's) greatness and power over the slave-master and his people, now Allah (God) attacks them at the height of their civilization and at the greatness of their power and strength, on the 4th of July...while they worship their greatness of their accomplishment; and the Black slave is sitting at his feet.

As it was with Nebuchadnezzar and as it was with Pharaoh, the same is being repeated today.

This is the significance of Allah's (God's) coming on the 4th of July. For four hundred years we have been suffering under the pangs of servitude - slavery and at the relentlessly merciless hands of the white slavemaster over us.

Allah (God) came to give justice and freedom to us and to make us equal members in the society of the new powerful, strong, and wise people of the earth.

Ever since that day, the 4th of July, 1930, has meant the doom of American domination over the Black man of America and the Black People of the earth. Ever since that day, America has been falling.

America's fall is not imminent...it is now going on. America refused to break her fall when she could have broken her fall, as the Bible teaches us. Babylon could have been healed, but she was not (Je. 51:9.). She did not do anything to warrant such forgiveness.

America has been offered the chance for forgiveness, but she refused to accept it, for she never offered to do anything favorable toward her Black slave, that would make them free of her power to rule them.

Black slaves went to their death, fighting the enemy

of the white slavemaster, to help America to maintain her independence against foreign dominance. The Black slave was not given anything in exchange for his sacrifice.

When a dog hunts for a hunter, the hunter(master) will sometimes share a part of the game with the dog. The Black slave has helped his master to overcome and to put other peoples under the control of his white slave-master. The Black slave has fought, bled and died around the earth, to help the white slave-master to conquer those whom the master called his enemies.

We helped the white man to conquer Cuba and to overcome and subdue Mexico and the Philippine Islands and other places around the earth, and also Japan. How many lives did the Black man lose in the Pacific while helping the white man to conquer the people of Japan who are the brown, half-brother of the Black man? The brown race and the yellow race are the half-brother of the Black man.

Whose independence? Now the white man and the Black man are both free on this day. The coming of Allah (God) on this day means the freedom of the Black man too.

The clear significance of Allah's (God's) coming on this day shows the great wisdom of Allah (God).

Everywhere the white man may be, even in Europe, the earth belongs to the Black man.

Let us rejoice on this day, the 4th of July, in the coming of Allah (God) Who came in the Person of Master Fard Muhammad to Whom praises are due forever and give thanks to Him.

Let us enjoy the independence he brought to us and the freedom, justice and equality.

He brought these things to us not by killing off the red Indian nor any original settlers. Justice and righteousness are the ammunition used by Allah (God).

CHAPTER 17

Independence

Independence means to be free of the dominance of others. It is a very happy feeling for one to enjoy self - freedom!

The white race, in the Western Hemisphere, takes this day, July 4, 1972, to be a day to worship in remembrance of their achieving Independence from other people.

The white race in the Western Hemisphere had to conquer the Indians who had an independent claim on the country now called America. Then the white race in America cut off the tie of England and France and became the independent holder of the present country called America, in the Western Hemisphere.

The white race was not satisfied with owning a new country to itself. They wanted the country built up but, the white man was afraid to trust himself to build the country up, so he goes to other countries that were civilized and uncivilized, Africa. From Africa he took our Black people as slaves and used us for hard-labor purposes.

Now, the white race has achieved those desires and now he has the glorious thing that man can enjoy—freedom. The country of America cannot be said to be the white man's own—but with having the freedom and the power to overcome the natives (Indians) of this country, the white race in America takes this day, July 4, to celebrate the joy of independence of others!

"As thou hast done so shall it be done unto thee." Someone is about to take away your enjoyable independence. The white race here in America has done the worse to the Black people who helped the white man to build up the country of America and to make it suitable and to bring in this enjoyable independence.

But the white race in America has angered God due to the evil done to us after our four hundred years, here, under the white race. The white race still desires to mistreat and to kill us all the day long.

The white man hates his Black slave; while the Black slave should be hating the white man, for mistreating the Black slave. But the white man made the Black slave to love him so well that when the white man mistreats him, the Black slave will not dislike the white man for mistreating him.

Now the time of God has arrived—the time that Allah (God) must separate the Black slave and his white slave master, and bring freedom to the Black slave.

So we see the power of our enemy being broken by God in destroying the power of the white man: power to maintain his sway over the whole world.

Independence is fine, if we can keep and maintain, independence! But there is a dark cloud of trouble now swinging over the country of America. The dark cloud makes her once freedom of thought and action become instead, a freedom of death, hell and destruction!

It is awful to think over the things of evil and of trouble that are coming upon the glorified North America.

The poor Black slave, numbering now into tens of millions of Black people, never knew anything of the joy of freedom, because the vicious enemy, like a young lion, as Daniel gives it in the Bible, has made the Black slave a prey to all of the white man's wicked desires.

Now, what do we have to celebrate in the fact that the white man is enjoying freedom over us? In celebrating the white man's independence, we make a fool out of ourselves. We cannot celebrate his day.

The only time that we the Black people have a day to worship and are able to call a day 'our day of freedom,' is when we are free from white America and free from any other nation, and become independent with some of this earth that we can call our own.

Then we can say that this is a freedom day and a holiday for us.

Black sisters, Black brothers, let us unite and get together and try and go from that which binds us to others.

CHAPTER 18

Slavery in Alabama and Mississippi

The white man's tricknology is always being trumpeted to the world (that they are peace lovers), as though they want all people, as they falsely claim, to be free and to live in peace, while they are sitting on and crushing between twenty and thirty million Black people in America, who were their servitude slaves a hundred years ago. Now, for one hundred years, the slavemasters' children falsely claim that we are free and that they are trying to treat us as free people.

It has come to me that in the state of Alabama, in Greene County, Alabama, there are big plantations owned by white people; and their stately white houses sit up on hills and the slaves live in a surrounding of shacks. These Black people work hard for very small pay. It is said by some that the salaries range from twenty-five cents a day to $2.50 a week. Rough clothes to work in are furnished to them.

This kind of slave labor goes on through the generations. One generation after another is subjected to this slave way of life in what is called a free world. In order to keep these Black people in this type of slavery, the owner has a mounted guard patrolling the plantation with a gun lying across his lap in the saddle on his horse, to see that there is no Black interference from the outside to entice the enslaved Blacks on the inside of his plantation to come in a better area for better wages.

These people grow up there and they die there on the plantation. Some of them never know civilization. They are satisfied because they know no other life but the slave life that their fathers and grandfathers have been living under. We hear this kind of slavery goes on not only in Greene County, Alabama, but in other states such as Mississippi and Georgia.

Years ago, when I was a young man in Georgia, I heard that such slavery on large plantations was going on in certain areas in Georgia. Our people will go to farm there (and the poor man probably owes another white farmer) and this white farmer pays the debt that he owes the other white farmer; and then the Black man becomes the slave the balance of his and his family's life on the plantation of this white man who paid the debt to a previous white plantation owner. As long as he lives, he never pays that debt. This is the worse injustice and the most cruel slavery of all.

They are shot and killed or beaten to death if they are found trying to leave the plantation. The white owners make other Blacks of the same plantation (under fear) be their informers of what is said and planned by other Blacks. It has been told to me in my younger life that certain rivers, lakes, and wooded wilderness-like places carry the bones and skulls of many Black slaves from these plantations in so called "freedom" times and in the age of abolished slavery by the law of this government and the world.

But in these southern states where Mr. George Wallace was running for president, he could make every Black man and woman in the south vote for him under fear.

These Black people are afraid to disobey white people in high offices or even an old white farmer who is hardly able to buy himself a new overall suit.

The Black people in the south have been brought up for many years and for centuries to fear white people. Where there is no freedom or chance to get out among free people, these Black people become the most ignorant and the most terrified people of whites that there are in the country of America. And the white man knows this. He gets rich. He builds himself a fine luxurious home on the plantation and as far as he can see he claims that the land is his and the poor slaves are living in the worst of shacks. When the rains come, some of them have to go to the walls of their houses with pails to catch the rain coming through their almost open roofs.

When winter comes, they are sitting up to their fireplaces trying to keep warm. These are the worst living conditions of human beings that could even be in the jungles of Africa where they do not have sawmills or brick kilns to saw timber into lumber and to mold bricks.

America has everything necessary to make her slaves good warm homes, cool homes, and to give her slaves a good living wage, because our fathers, for four hundred years, have already supplied the wealth for us today to be given good, substantial wages for our necessities of life.

It is pitiful to go in these southern areas, out in the rural districts, and see how, after four hundred years, the wicked, sun burned, keen-nosed, tobacco juice-mouthed, and blue eyed-devils are buckling our poor people down to such slavery conditions; crushing them to death, and diseasing them. Their children are coming up suffering from malnutrition. Fever and other diseases capture them and take them to their crude pine box graves or to a hole in the ground in the south. Without anything like honor of their death, they are buried in rough pine wooden boxes.

The Black man of America is so mistreated by his four hundred year old slave master and his slavemasters' children that you just cannot describe any other mistreatment of human beings to equal the evil and ill treatment that the Black Man has and still suffers in America.

In many towns and cities of the Southern states (even in their capitols) you will find the Black Man living in a very bad condition. His toilet is sometimes an open boarded up place, stinking right there in the city and diseasing the citizens because of that evil demon,   the white man, who wants to give all the ill he can to a people who have served him as slaves for four hundred years. This is going on in the South. Go see it for yourself.

The U.S. Mail comes into these towns and cities and in some places the Black people are forced to walk to a drug store and ask a white drug store owner for their mail. Then they are treated like dogs and as though the white devils are giving him something free while the senders of the mail have paid tax for postal carriers to bring it to their doors.

Little Black children are walking around with sores—pus running out of them—for the lack of medical attention. Little Black children are dying of diseases right in the false "freedom" of the U.S.A.

The Black people are cowered down by this vicious enemy who keeps his gun loaded to blow them down. An every happy, one-sided, grinning-mouthed policeman or sheriff is seeking ust the slightest chance to kill a Negro. He only has to say to his brother devil judge that he 'had to kill a Negro' and the judge looks at him and gives him a big smile and a hand clasp as though he did not kill enough ("you ought to kill all of them").

I have heard from their mouths, when I lived in the South, that "there were too many Negroes in the South and the white people should kill off some of them." "There are more Negroes than whites and the white man should kill off some of these Negroes." What chance does the Black man have under the shadow of the American government for freedom, justice and equality?

I thank Allah in the Person of Master Fard Muhammad, to Whom praise is due forever, who has come to deliver the Black man in America and to kill our oppressors.

This is very good, and we should be shouting day and night that a deliverer has come. The revelation of the Bible has given this people the right name (a beast), and a most vicious description does the revelation give. In Daniel of the Bible, this people is described as a beast rising up out of the sea with three ribs of a man in its mouth. This is the description of America with the Black slaves swallowed for three centuries in the power of our enemies (the devils).

The Black Man of the South would be a fool to vote for any white man of the South to rule him. He should stay away from the polls, because the white man for whom he votes is an enemy of his and is bound to tighten the shackles tighter than ever. They preach of enforcing the law, and that law is an unjust law directed against the Black Man.

Vote for Allah and for His servant, Elijah Muhammad and by the power of our Allah (God), who has come in the Person of Master Fard Muhammad, to Whom praise is due forever, all the prophecies of the Bible of what He will do in freeing the Black man of America will be fulfilled.

Let us submit to Him and live in peace with money, in good homes, and with the friendship of God and the righteous. There is nothing that you have to fear today, but God Himself. It is useless for us to fear our enemy after the coming and presence of our God, Who has power over the very atoms of life; for it is fear of the white man that will cause our people to eat the fire of hell with the white man if they do not recognize the fact that it is God Whom they should fear and not the devil. The world of the white man is now crumbling and coming to naught. The safety of the Black man is in His God. As the Holy Qur'an teaches us, in this day and time, seek refuge in Allah, the God of the Black man. He is the only place of refuge.

We have made America one of the richest and strongest people on earth. Her mighty navy is commanding the high seas with undersea craft crawling on the bottom of the ocean, carrying deadly weapons to surface and pour out on towns and cities of other than America and with listening devices set up throughout the earth on land, sea, and in the air, to listen to see what people are saying about her and planning against her, knowing she is guilty and deserving of death, and that she should be taken and destroyed.

She has prepared to put up a mighty battle, but Allah too has prepared and He is the Best Preparer; knowing their thoughts before they were ever made.

They have not the slightest chance today against the power of Allah that is working against them, even through the forces of nature.

The white race has been disgracing the entire Black nation of the earth. Africa is suffering under the same wicked power of the white race and having an awful time trying to rid herself of such a demon. She will do so — and soon.

Here in America, Almighty Allah (God) wants to make himself known with both the punishment and the destruction of this mighty, powerful, and rich people.

Fear not, my dear Black people, for we have Allah with us; and He is a mighty, a strong, and the most powerful one to be feared. Come follow me, and I will lead you to your salvation.

CHAPTER 19

Alabama

According to an article in the November 25, 1969, issue of **The-Wall Street Journal,** written by Mr. Neil Maxwell, staff reporter, and according to the reports of our own farmers, the Muslim property and lives are being attacked by a devil, Mr. James H. Bishop, who calls himself a missionary. He has started attacking us for a fight.

The Muslims have lost a couple of head of cattle by gun-shot perpetrated by some coward, according to the report of Mr. Neil Maxwell.

This demon, Mr. James H. Bishop seeks to bring himself and the American people into a war with Allah (God) and the righteous, which will be the end of America and her people.

We, the Muslims, are a people of peace and have and are proving ourselves to be just that all over America. And of course this demon, Mr. James H. Bishop, is proving himself to be just what he is made to be, a mischief-maker, as Allah (God) Who came in the Person of Master Fard Muhammad, to Whom praises are due forever has taught me that he is.

I will warn this troublemaker that he is playing with fire, and a very hot fire; for he is not attacking Elijah Muhammad and his followers; but he is attacking Allah (God) Who welcomes the attack for this is what He came for.

As sure as Allah (God) lives, we will convert every Black man in America to his or her own, and this includes those in Alabama.

Look at the Muslims' condition in Alabama. We went there to buy a piece of land from a citizen of Alabama and then some white enemy appeared who calls himself a preacher of the gospel of Jesus; but he did not forget to preach the gospel of the devil along with it. This devil, Mr Bishop — we hired him when we first went to the farm in Alabama. He worked for us on the farm digging holes to help us to get set up on the farm. At that time he said nothing to us in the way of charging us with being there illegally. Why did he hire out to us? Why did he help us to get started on our farm? We hired him and paid him for his work and there was no talk from him in the manner in which he is talking now.

So this man has now turned to be a real open enemy and not a secret enemy. He even goes so far now to even talk of killing us and is asking us for a fight. We are losing cattle from bullet wounds and he is speaking in the direction of even destroying our property and cattle. He even makes it hard for us to buy gasoline; and the most ignorant and worst thing is that the gas-attendant sells us the gasoline; anp then we are arrested and charged with a crime for buying the gasoline, instead of charging the man who sold it to us. It is very ignorant and silly.

We have bought land and cattle in Alabama. We mean to get the profit out of what we bought and if the government of Alabama intends to drive us out from our property they will have to buy us out; not drive us out.

If the government of Alabama is in agreement with the white people of Alabama in what they are doing against the Muslims, then I want to say to the whole of white America that we have Allah (God) on our side to retaliate against anyone who mistreats us. We did not go down there with rifles and guns to shoot anyone. We are Muslims and the brother of Muslims. If we are not accepted by our brother Muslims, we most certainly have been accepted by the God of Islam, Allah, Whose Proper Name is Master Fard Muhammad, to Whom Praises are due forever, Who came to us without observation, as it is written of Him, however He makes His work manifest. The Nation of Islam's idea again is to build better country homes for the Black people.

I say to the whole of the American white people that you could never win against anyone outside or inside of America as long as you seek to mistreat us. As it is written in the Bible, 'He who contends with thee (us) Allah (God) Will Contend with him and give them their blood to drink like sweet wine."

So remember, we are the people of Allah (God). We make no trouble with anyone, but Allah (God) Will retaliate against anyone who makes trouble for us, or who seeks to do us harm....

CHAPTER 20

Decline of the Dollar

The strong-hold of the American Government is falling to pieces. She has lost her prestige among the nations of the earth. One of the greatest powers of America was her dollar. The loss of such power will bring any nation to weakness, for this is the media of exchange between nations. The English pound and the American dollar have been the power and beckoning light of these two great powers. But when the world went off the gold and silver standard, the financial doom of England and America was sealed.

The pound has lost 50 percent of its value. America's dollar has lost everything now as power backing for her currency, which was once backed by gold for every $5 note and up. All of her currency was backed by silver, from a $1 note up.

But today, the currency of America is not backed by any sound value—silver or gold. The note today is something that the government declares they will give you the value in return, but does not name what that value is. But they definitely are not backing their currency with silver or gold.

This is the number-one fall, and it is very clear that the loss of the power of the American dollar means the loss of the financial power of America. What will happen since there is no sound backing for her notes we do not know.

What should we expect even in the next twelve months under the fall of the power of America's dollar? This means that we have 100 percent inflation. What could happen under 100 percent inflation? Your guess is as good as mine. The power of gold and silver was once abundant in America. But the touch of the finger of God against the power of so mighty a nation has now caused the crumbling and fall of America.

We can easily and truthfully liken the fall of America to the prophetic symbolical picture given in the (Bible) Revelation of John 18:2. The name Babylon used there does not really say whether it is ancient Babylon or a picture of some future Babylon.

The description it gives is as follows:

"And he (angel) cried mightily with a strong voice (with authority) saying, Babylon the great is fallen, is fallen and is become the habitation of devils, (Allah has declared the people to be a race of devils) and the hole of every foul spirit and a cage of every unclean and hateful bird." The description here give to the Babylon by the prophets compares with the present history and people of America and their fall.

The picture shows the cause of her fall. Number one, she had become the habitation of devils, and being the habitation of devils makes her a haven for every people that love the works and doings of the devil. Here the prophet refers to them, symbolically, as being a hole of every foul spirit, and a cage of every unclean and hateful bird.

People are referred to as birds, snakes, beasts, fish and other animals to tell or represent the characteristics of that person. It is universally known that the very beginning of the American people was from the lower class of European people. And their first ruler (President Washington) was a fugitive from England. And the common, dissatisfied and lower grade of European people followed and boosted his authority. This filled and inhabited America with a very low class and low-based people.

And then this type of people went into Africa and purchased slaves from among our people who were also uneducated, most of them; but there were a few who were highly educated. All of these began to mix with the low-based, evil-minded, real citizens of the Western Hemisphere (whites). And when America began to get strong in power, she opened her doors to the underprivileged (laborers) in overpopulated countries such as China, Japan, and in Europe to seek citizenship in America.

This brought into America one of the most mixed people, who were granted the freedom to live any kind of life they chose. They were not forced to serve the God of the universe who made heaven and earth nor any religion. They had freedom of worship. This made America a haven for any people who wished to be free of the compellers of religious and just rule and authority. This people for the past five hundred years have put into practice every evil that is imaginable.

The freedom of uncleanliness is granted and is worshipped. The percentage of sexual worship of the same sex is greater than any government on the face of the earth. Little children are being taught sex almost from the cradle, making the whole nation, as one man put it, "nearly 90 percent freaks of nature."

It is common to see on the streets of any metropolitan city of America men sweethearting with men and women sweethearting with women. Little boys with boys and little girls with girls.

It is common that a decent family is puzzled as to where to send their children for schooling. There are no all-girl schools as there once were. They are all girl schools of sweethearts; the same sex falling upon their own. Boys' colleges are breeding such filthy practice; the jail houses, prisons, and the federal penitentiaries are all breeding dens of homosexuals.

As the Prophet says in the 18th chapter: "She is a cage of every unclean and hateful bird." There are types of hateful birds. This is why a symbolical name is given. It means human beings. There are birds of prey and birds that are unclean such as crows, owls, buzzards and ravens who live and thrive off the carcass of others. And there are unclean people living and thriving off the unclean.

It is time that God intervenes to bring about an end of such people as the wicked of America. She offers the same filth to all of the civilized of the earth, and she hates you if you are against her way of life and will threaten you with death as the Sodomites did Lot and his followers. But I say to you as the 4th verse of Revelations, Chapter 18 says: You that want to be a better people than this, "come out of her."

The so-called American Negroes are referred to here in the 4th verse as being God's people ("My people") Come out of her...that ye be not partakers of her sins and that ye receive not of her plagues."

This is a call to the American so-called Negroes to give up a doomed, wicked people that has destroyed them from being a people worthy of recognition, and who have now become lovers of their enemies and destroyers.

The 5th verse tells us that "Her sins have reached into heaven and God has remembered her iniquities and is ready to destroy her." Her destruction cometh quickly, according to the 8th verse, that plagues of death, mourning and famines which cometh in one day (one year) then after that she shall be destroyed by fire, utterly burned.''

This is backed up in these words: ''Strong is the Lord God who judge her.'' Here it gives us a knowledge that He who judges is well able with power, with wisdom, and with deliberate and careful maneuvering to make judgment against her.

CHAPTER 21

Destruction of America's Education

The plague of Allah (God) against the educational system of America is something that the philosophers and scientists should look into, as the destruction of America's education is the destruction of their wisdom to educate the people.

There are many who look on the destruction without taking a second thought of the destruction of America's education. Education is a guide for the people to keep and maintain a civilized life. It is education that civilizes us. Now to see the citizens of America rebelling against the American educational system is something that the wise of the wise should take thought of.

The American people actually have come to the point where they hate their own educational system. This means that they are now hating and destroying their civilization because it is education that civilizes people.

The American people no longer want their education and they are destroying the very houses that house their text books of education. They are rebelling against their teachers who teach education. They are fighting their teachers and then they set their houses on fire — schools, colleges and universities. This means in words, as I have said above, that they are destroying their own civilization.

The Black people of today who are blindly helping the white people to destroy this civilization are like Samson was in his day and time; he helped to pull the building down, but he was blind to the effect of the destruction of the building. All Samson wanted to do was to get even with his mockers who had put out his eyes and who laughed at him. Samson did not care whether there would be a civilization left behind him or not. He was willing to die, blind to the knowledge of the future of his people and those people he was destroying.

Throughout America, her colleges, her universities and her teachers are in danger. The students no longer want old world guidance. It is a new world that they want. But in their mad destruction of the old world they do not know how to prepare for a new world civilization. They do not have guidance for a new civilization, and in their madness they refuse to hear a teacher teaching of an educational system of a better civilization...the civilization of the Black man.

The wisdom of the educational system of the aboriginal Black Man of the earth has never been known to this world because the Black man was put to sleep in order to let this world (white man) try itself at ruling. Now the rule of this world has been found to be dissatisfying and the dissatisfaction is 100 per cent.

Allah (God) has come to take over and to guide another people into setting up a better educational system for the people of whom He Himself is the Head. And we all get guidance from Him, as Daniel said in his prophecy, "God will set up a kingdom and He will not leave it into the hands of others, but He Himself will guide it." But first He must remove all the rubbish of this white man's world educational system. He discards America's educational system, as we discard rubbish to be burned up.

The Black man who hears the teachings of Islam

feels proud that he has been taught something that he has wished for all of his life. But the average Black man that hears does not accept it as he should. He accepts it in such way that he can be criticized and mocked; for he wants to take a piece of it, as he has done in the past and he runs away with it claiming that he knows this. He will try to set up something of his own from a few words of it. This throws the Black man behind. They do this through envy, jealousy, and proudness on the part of the person. This is the way the Black man of America is divided. The devil knows that the Black man is proud and envious. The white man helps him to be this way so that the Black man will never get any place towards self, if the Black man takes such steps to divide himself up.

Look how the devil is teaching our people division now. The devil goes and gets everyone whom he thinks of for the Black people to idolize them. Look at how he names streets after Rev. Martin Luther King and Malcolm because he was the devil's disciple. Rev. Martin Luther King was not the disciple of the Black man. He preached integration with white people and become white folk, and then the white man killed him. The white man does the same to you, although you follow what the white man tells you to follow and you worship the white man.

Many times, I have reminded you that Rev. Martin Luther King was not trying to separate you from the enemy, but instead he was trying to unite you with the enemy. Rev. Martin Luther King was not seeking a home for you as Moses was seeking a home for Israel who was opposed in Egypt. In modern day America, I am seeking an independent home for you. Rev. Martin

Luther King did not do this. Rev. Martin Luther King taught you to submit to the white man and to become one of them. All of your life you have known that this is destruction—after so-called freedom. It is the same as the dog returning to his vomit. The Black man was vomited out of the white man and now goes back to the white man...

The white man is right when he says that you are free. You are free; but if you go back to him for him to put chains on you again, he will do so.

Malcolm fell out from us a hypocrite. He went and joined white people and worshiped them and he got what he preached for. Now the white man names colleges after Malcolm only to get you to join in the philosophy which he left behind; that white people are good. Malcolm went to Mecca and saw white people. And instead of joining in with the Black Man, he joined in with the white man, although he was taught the white man's birth and death. He preached it as long as he did not turn enemy against me. He turned enemy against me, for he wanted my place over the people and he thought that by going over the earth and making a mockery of me, he would do just that...get rid of me. But the very people of Mecca and Egypt and other places he went, they are with me today. Here, in the United States of America, today, I have more followers than I had before Malcolm said a word.

You cannot disgrace one whom Allah (God) has taken for His friend, for He has the power to keep your disgrace to a naught. The white man teaches you to worship Malcolm in order to lead you astray against me. You come around trying to argue with us.

I do not give two cents for you following Malcolm if you want to follow him. You will get divine death and destruction with no one to give you any honor and respect...only the devil whom you serve. The devil sets enemies and hypocrites for you to worship in order to pull you away from me. He knows that you would be a fool to follow enemies and hypocrites. But that is to turn you away from your salvation which I am preaching. You cannot prosper fighting against me, for Allah (God) is not with you; He is with Me. It does not matter how many devils you have with you, you could have a world full of devils, but that would not amount to anything. It shows how anxious you are to get what the devil offers you for following his guidance. Allah (God) came to put an end to the enemy devil and their power to rule. This you will learn.

I am not without power from Allah (God) by any means, regardless to whether everyone of you rejects following me. I mean the whole thirty million of you. That will not stop me or condemn me as being not able to lead you. You Black people in America are no more than a small family. We have a world of Black people that I can continue to teach, and they are anxious for me to come and teach them. After I teach you the truth, it is immaterial to me whether or not you believe and follow me.

If all the little Black organizations who are trying to do something for self would unite with me and make a complete body of one, we will most certainly have salvation in our hands at once. If we all want to be like Christianity, with each one sitting and enjoying his little part... in one day they will lose their part.

The destruction of America's educational system is the best thing that Allah (God) could do to get rid of that which you depend on for guidance. America's educational system has never benefitted you and me, only to keep us slaves to the white man. We the Black people want an educational system that will bring us into unity as a man before Allah (God). We want an educational system that we can read in the light of ancient and modern history. We want an educational system that will guide us through tomorrow — not an educational system that is dying today. What hope can you have in a world that is crashing and bursting asunder as America is? Do you think that we will be here, and that you will go back like you were before the war? I say you wait and see.

This is the end of America. Allah (God) will destroy her for she is the most evil one of the white race. America is more evil than Europe. America is worse than her father, England.

Look what is going on at the present time, day and night. Black man, America has no respect for you, nor for your woman; yet you desire America's civilization; and still you want to destroy it. Now what do you want my dear man? I think that you should first prepare to replace that which you are destroying. I advise you to unite with me and let us build a nation like a single house. A united force is always better than a divided one.

I say unite with me, for I cannot unite with you; for you do not have anything for me to unite with you for. You have nothing but a chain carrying it around that any wise civilized man can take and bind you with continuously.

You may be able to wreck the whole of America, but you have nothing to replace it with. "Vengeance is Mine saith the Lord, I will repay." Look how He is repaying America with rain, snow, hail, earthquakes...these can destroy America at once, but He brings her destruction upon her gradually. As the Holy Qur'an teaches, "Allah (God) brings them (wicked) to a naught little by degrees from whence they (wicked) cannot perceive."

Allah (God) came to give you better names that have a better meaning, a greater meaning, an eternal meaning. These names of Allah (God) will live forever. But the names of the white man will not live forever. Allah (God) offers you and me heaven at once ..not heaven after you are dead. If we do not accept heaven he can also put us in hell if we reject His help.

Remember the destruction of America's educational system means the doom of America. You are not left to wander aimlessly. The Holy Qur'an plainly teaches you and me that Allah (God) would not lead you to wander aimlessly. Allah (God) has that aim and purpose to you, in me...so come and follow me and learn the new education for the Black man is not designed for you, the Black man in America alone; it is for Black people all over the earth. Take it or leave it.

CHAPTER 22

Savagery of America

The great country of America and her great richness, great institutions, and her great towns and cities, spread out like a blanket over the surface of the Western Hemisphere with her tall buildings going upward over a hundred stories! The great architects and building engineers have become such experts at building to precision that it makes their past history of two and four thousand years ago look like child's play.

Her land is shadowed with the wings of her many planes which cover her almost like a cloud. The great and wonderful work of science on the earth and in the air, her great mighty fleets afloat on the high seas (on the surface and below the surface), her great scientific mechanical communications system! Yet with all of this might of skill in engineering or building, the country of America displays and practices more savagery than any civilized country on the earth. And all of her educational institutions are not enough to make a man so intelligent and proud of his education and of being an American citizen that he would not practice the same savagery.

There is no such thing as law and order. The law is disregarded, as though it were thrown in the jungles to be carried out by savage beasts. Murdering, killing, robbery, raping, and drug addiction are the only law and order that is respected.

It has become such a country that the civilized man of intelligence and decency is afraid to walk the streets of the vast towns and cities of America. He would be more secure in the jungles, around and in the midst of wild beasts than to be walking in the streets of these great cities in America after night.

Groups of robbers and murderers, killers, and dope addicts are prowling the streets after night to exact their evil intentions upon the innocent. This is a mob of savages that the intelligent and decent woman should not dare venture out among. And if we see such women walking around, they are part of this savage people.

It has become dangerous even for the girl and woman to be standing alone in any unprotected place, day or night. Rapists lurking around bus stations and robbers also and thieves are at such stations, and with such conditions existing in a so-called civilized country like America, this is the worst name that could be applied to her.

Police, detectives, and FBI all are here; but these daring savage acts are committed right before their eyes and ears.

CHAPTER 23

The Dissatisfied

We are living in the time when dissatisfaction is 100 per cent throughout the world of man and mankind. Therefore we are living among the dissatisfied persons, daily and nightly.

No one is satisfied though they may be righteous. They are not satisfied because they are living among unrighteousness. So the whole entire world of the wicked and the righteous is upset due to dissatisfaction.

The dissatisfied are gaining everyday more and more among the people whom they hope to bring into the same condition that they are in. And today nothing is made so clear to the chief-maker of dissatisfaction.

The Black people in North America, who are up from slavery, are the target of the white slave-masters' children who wish to keep them here and deprived of their salvation, if possible. The white man holds out promises to the Black man only to deceive the Black man. The white man fascinates the Black man and tries to do that for the Black man that the white man does not want to do. But nevertheless, he does these things in order to get his hold on the Black once-slave; to go to the white man's doom with him. The devil is the open enemy of the original Black people of the earth.

Temptation — The white man is trying to tempt the Black man all over the earth to take part with the white man in evil and filth. Here in America, if you will bear me witness, sex talk is the topic of conversation   twenty-four hours a day on the radio and the television. These public broadcasts to the people contain some of the most filthy talk and some of the most filthy actions on the screen than we ever dreamed of hearing from a neighbor even in private...not to think of in public.

The Black man in America is on the radio twenty-four hours a day. The white man loves to weigh the Black People out in his filthy language of sex to see how many of our Black People he can get to go to hell with the white man by persuading them with his sexual talk. The Holy Quran is 100 percent right. Read it, and try and find something in there that is not true. If you think that you have found something come to me and I will show you and the world that it is true.

Black man, this is the end of the rule of the white man. Allah (God) came to Kill them for mistreating the Black once-slave here in America. Allah (God) says in Isaiah (Bible) that He will kill our enemy and call us by another Name. Black Brother, this is going on right in your eyes, but you still think that the time is prolonged to the distant future and that you will not live to see it. But, I say to you all, in truth, that you are living in it now.

The scientists of America know that America is on her way out. And since you, Black man, are the righteous, perhaps all of you will be saved; for you are bound to submit when you see what is coming. Allah (God) will take you and me and call us after His own name. As I haved preached to you for years, as long as we go in the name of the white man we are his people to serve him and to go to his doom with him.

The white man is stripping you of decent clothes to

wear. Many of you come out in the public one-half nude. He is making you shameless. You are doing something that you did not know you would ever be able to do. But, it is in you, that you would like to obey the devil and not obey Allah (God), the God of righteousness, truth, freedom, justice and equality. It is so shameful for you to sit and let your voices be heard on the radio and television answering the filthy questions that the white man is asking concerning your own personal self and the way that you think.

The white man is only trying to choose you to go to hell with him. That white man knows that there is no heaven for him. There will be a remnant of them saved, but the majority are going down and they are taking a fighting chance of it in the way of deceiving you to go along with them. That is the reason both Books, the Bible and the Holy Qur'an, teach us not to let the archdeceiver deceive us.

But the devil is doing it night and day. Why do you think he has these twenty-four hour talk shows talking among you and with you, if it is not to get you to agree with them so that you will go along with them to their doom?

Certainly they hate me and the Muslims who follow me. But their hatred does not make any difference with us, just as long as Allah (God) does not hate us. Their hatred goes for nothing if Allah (God) is not hating us. As it is written, "He whom Allah Befriends is not disgraced." Allah (God) has always backed up His people, who are of the righteous and who believe in Him from ancient time, until this day.

Fear not. Lift up your heads in the pride of truth and love for you Black man and the God of the Black man.

The dissatisfied must be removed from the satisfied of Allah (God) and His people of righteousness. The lost-found Black aboriginal people in America have the greatest gift coming to them of any people who lived in the past. They will have a new growth put into them and they will be changed in the twinkling of an eye, as it is written in the Bible and in the Holy Qur'an. This change will take place after Satan has been conquered and cast out of the earth from among the aboriginal Black people to whom the white man is no kin.

CHAPTER 24

Confusion, Confusion of People

Now the rise of America's once slave into the knowledge of self, in the spirit of Allah, in the Person of Master Fard Muhammad (the son of Man), the Author of the Resurrection of us the mentally dead is causing untold confusion among the heads of state.

The scripture is being fulfilled wherein it prophesies that in these days (meaning the end of the wicked world of Satan), rulers are against rulers—kings against kings. In the days of the prophets, there were no heads of government who were given the name president. Rulers were referred to as rulers and as kings of the people.

The prediction of the prophets, who wrote our future before we lived is now coming to pass. The slaves (or a foolish people, as they are referred to by Moses) are vexing the slave master. Today, as these prophecies are now being fulfilled, we are not surprised at the truth God gave to us through the mouths of His prophets coming to pass, as it was prophesied.

The master must give up his slave and the slave must give up his master, regardless of his desire to remain with his master. It is the purpose of God, Himself to separate the two so that He can give the slave justice and equal chance for survival, as the slave master has been exercising power over the slave.

America is being torn to pieces politically as Pharaoh's political party was in the days when Jehovah went after the freedom of Israel.

Egypt was plagued with droughts, great hail

storms, rain, and fire, according to the Psalms, running side-by-side (fire and water). These plagues now are visiting America from Almighty Allah (God).

Our people, who have no knowledge of the Book and scriptures, can make grave errors in trying to continue with the old world of the Black man's enslavers and enslavement.

There are many of our people — especially among yesterday's leadership—who desire to lead the shackled slave into more secure shackles for the sake of the master and for the fear of the master's dislike of the leadership.

This is found among the spiritual leaders more than among the political leaders of Black America, which makes manifest to you that the spiritual leadership fears not the God of truth and justice, but fears the enemy of God (God is the author of freedom, justice and equality of man).

We must have unity with the Black Nation of the earth, of which you and I are members, and who are leaving in search of us, since now having the knowledge that we were bound in the chains of slavery in the Western Hemisphere of our earth. We cannot come forth, making the steps of freedom towards a free people, until the shackles have been cut to allow our steps to be made freely.

It is written so plainly in the last book of the Bible that the fearful and the unbelieving leadership and their followers of the enemy (the beast)—and the scripture does not try to hide giving the slave master one of the worst names, as he is like a savage beast against the Black man of America and the world (people of God)—shall go down with the beast in a lake of fire.

Our unity with God, Who has already appeared among us in the Person of Master Fard Muhammad, to Whom praise is due forever, will set us in heaven while we live and on this earth, our national home.

CHAPTER 25

America's Loss of Friendship

Bible, Obad. 15, "...As thou has done, it shall be done unto thee." America has done the worst work of deceiving other peoples and making false friendships with them. Now her turn has come. No one wants to trust her for friendship, for she has deceived many nations.

Rev. Ch. 12 (Bible) prophesies of America under the worst names that could be given to a human being: serpent, snake, Satan, devil, and the deceiver of the people of the earth. Therefore, the Black man is warned in Rev. 18:4, "...Come out of her, my people..." This scripture warns the Black man to give up Babylon, which is a symbolic name, meaning America. America has tormented the Black Man. Now a tormentor is after her. The Divine Tormentor, says that we should not be partakers of the divine torment coming against America from Allah (God) Who came in the Person of Master Fard Muhammad, to Whom praises are due forever. This means, "separation." We must separate ourselves from America so that we will be saved from the stroke of the Master Who Is God Himself. Allah (God) is whipping America with all kinds of calamities.

I have been writing for many years that America must be punished for her evil done to her Black once-slaves, who are so-called free-slaves now, and who continue to suffer the same, or worse, punishment under the children of the white slave master, than their white fathers imposed upon our Black fathers under servitude-slavery.

America has not only lost and is still losing friendship all over Asia and Africa, ...but she is now losing friendship right here with her next-door neighbors, Central and South America.

The manner—the ill-treatment and dislike with which they received the President's Fact-Finding Committee—made it seem as though they should have been on the other side of the earth. Steps had to be taken to protect their physical self in a country which is right next-door to America.

However, the scripture must be fulfilled; they shall eat America's bread and burn her body with fire.

I quote from Rev. 17:16, "And the ten horns which thou sawest upon the beast, these shall hate the whore... and shall eat her flesh, and burn her with fire!" The 'horns' here are a symbolic reference to Central and South America (America's satellites).

This means that America's gifts and what-not will be accepted, but this does not mean that America has bought their sincere friendship. They will take all the gifts which America offers, but still this does not mean that America has their heart.

America is careful not to give any help to her Black once-slave for four hundred years to do something for themselves. America wants to keep her Black slave tied while she watches their movements.

If we go to her asking America for a territory so that we can live to ourselves, she turns a deaf ear to us. We helped America for hour hundred years, in every respect as though we were one-half owners of the country. We have gotten nothing in return but beatings, cheatings and shootings down on the highway.

If we think that there is a God of Mercy (and there is One)...should we not think that He will sympathize with the poor Black slave to receive justice from his master?

The Black slave helped to make America rich. Would Allah, (God) be silent forever? Being the God of Righteousness and Justice, would He not take to Himself the work of aiding the poor Black people against their evil oppressors?

America wants everyone to help her bemoan all of her set-backs; but when she causes others to fall...breaks up the countries of other peoples and destroys their independence and freedom, she laughs and prides herself as doing a great thing. She puts her feet upon their economic neck and destroys their independence as a nation.

All this now returns to America. The little nations are now awake. They had looked for true friendship from America but instead America deceived them.

Again, I repeat, the Bible prophecy..."As thou has done, it shall be done unto thee." There is no friend for America. Also it is written in the Bible, "In the day of thy fall, none shall help thee...."

Why? Because you, America, have been and are an aide of the destruction and fall of other peoples. So who should help you in the day of your fall? This is what Allah (God) wants to bring home to America through His prophets.

The Holy Qur'an refers to America in this kind of prophecy: "When her doom comes there will come one calamity after another." As soon as she thinks she is getting over the sore made by a previous calamity, another will attack her.

America is undergoing all that is prophesied against her. It is nothing new. It is well-known.

We have been eating the bread of affliction and suffering the poisonous bites of our white slave master. It has caused actual death of our proper mental way of thinking. The natural brain of the Black slave is poisoned and cannot think for itself.

So Allah (God) is asking us to separate from white America. But the mentally dead do not want to go from her for they have not yet gotten the knowledge of truth of our God, Allah and His Mercy for them.

The Black - slave - children are victimized by the white slavemaster, because of the condition the white slave-master brought our Black slave-fathers up in. They do not readily hear the right answer to the problem. Regardless, to how I cry in their midst, they are poisoned and mentally dead.

CHAPTER 26

Will America Repent?

This is a great question. America knows her evil-doings against us; but to repent of it, I doubt it much. She feels that if she tries to make up with us for her evil-doing to us, she would be inviting her disgrace among the nations of the earth. Her determination is to try and keep the so-called Negroes from believing in the true God, Allah, and the true religion of Islam, which is our salvation. They are using many tricks now to deceive the so-called Negroes. The foolish so-called Negroes are falling for them.

False friendship is not able to stand up for very long; an enemy is just not able to put over false friendship for long. You should be able to know them and their tricks as long as they have been putting them over on you.

According to the Holy Qur'an (60:1), friendly relations with enemies of Islam is forbidden. "O, you who believe, do not take my enemy and your enemy for friends: Would you offer them love while they deny what has come to you of the truth, driving out the apostle and yourselves because you believe in Allah, your Lord?"

In this kind of doings, the foolish so-called Negroes will be trapped. There are even some weak Muslims who ignore this warning. Some even go as far as to marry the enemies of Islam, and they even hate me for teaching the truth of the enemies. But Allah is with me, and I have no right to worry about the doings of the people after knowledge. The enemy does not love either you or me. As the next verse teaches: "If they find you, they will be your enemies, and will stretch forth towards you their hands and their tongues with evil, and they ardently desire that you may disbelieve." "They would slay you with their hands, and speak evil to and of you with their tongues."

You must remember that you do not like one who befriends your enemy. How much does God dislike you for making love with His enemies? The enemy does not have to be a real devil. He could be your father, mother, brother, husband, wife or children. Many times they're of your own household. Today is the great time of the separation of the righteous Muslims and the wicked white race.

The wicked are not by any means asleep to the knowledge of the time. They are really on the job of truth. You must know the truth whether you accept it or reject it! Ask yourself these questions:

(1) If Christianity is the religion of Jesus, why is it that the wicked (white race) represents it, instead of the righteous or holy people of the East (Islam)? (2) Why has not the Holy City Mecca allowed it to be taught within her? (3) Why is not Jerusalem the capital of Christianity instead of Rome, Italy? (4) If Christianity was the religion of Jesus and the white race is Jesus' beloved people, why did He preach the "doom" of the white race and the coming of a new world?

This people will most certainly carry to their doom many of our people because of our peoples' fear and love of them. Look out of your door or window; see the Black woman sitting in the car close in the arms of your and her enemy. The enemy does not love her. He only wants to disgrace her and you and keep her from seeing the hereafter. You cannot have any such freedom with his women, and especially not in front of his door. Love of them will get you the hell.

CHAPTER 27

The Troubled America: No Peace

America, in trying to hold her place as the greatest power among the nations of earth, is one of the most troubled countries on earth today.

The world has never before seen the top rulers of the land leaving their offices to visit nations abroad. The purpose of these visits to foreign countries is to make peace with them after years of troubling them.

America brought all of her troubles upon herself. She alone is to be charged with being the cause of the troubled world and people today.

America loves meddling into other people's affairs. She just cannot stay out of other people's business, whether they be a two-cents worth soap-box teacher or presidents and kings of countries.

America's actions fit the description of the prophecy (Bible) "The beast has eyes around about." This refers to the mechanical listening devices with which America listens in on other people's private affairs, as well as her listening in on foreign governmental affairs. This also refers to her powerful telescope.

America goes abroad and makes war against other people. Then she charges them with making war against her when she is the one who is guilty of the war-making.

The Bible says Allah (God) will destroy those who delight themselves in making war.

CHAPTER 28

Is Modern America as Merciless as Ancient Ninevah

"Woe to the bloody city! It is all full of lies and robbery; the prey departeth not; The noise of a whip, and the noise of the rattling of the wheels, and of the prancing horses, and of the jumping chariots." (Nahum 3:1,2)

America answers this prophecy of the ruins of ancient Ninevah. Ninevah was full of lies and robbery; so is America. "The prey departeth not." The poor so-called Negroes in America are the prey and they refuse to depart from America regardless of the evil treatment they receive. Though the whips and the clubs of their enemy are heard night and day upon the heads and backs of the prey (so-called Negroes), they still do not desire to depart from America.

Ancient Ninevah, according to her history, was full of chariots that made much noise and the prancing horses carrying the chariots in full speed that the prophets described them as "jumping chariots." So it is in America today: her cities are filled with automobiles and the noise of them is heard every hour of the day, rattling past our doors.

She is full of blood from murdered people. She also fills another prophecy made in Habakkuk 2:12: "Woe to him that buildeth a town with blood, and stablisheth a city by iniquity!"

America was founded and built with blood and established by iniquity. She killed the aboriginal inhabitants (Indians) to establish herself as an independent people at the great loss of lives of the original owners. Her great progress has been made by the work of iniquity. She has robbed many people; and the blood of her slaves, the so-called Negroes, has stained the earth here and elsewhere, slain by her hands.

The lawless people kill their own leaders and assassinate their rulers. Anyone who opens his mouth for justice for the poor prey (so-called Negroes) is seized, prosecuted, and in many cases slain because he dared open his mouth for the oppressed against the oppressors.

Woe to America! She has established a government with blood. The murderers seek to kill the innocent all the day long. Regardless of the people's choice of a ruler, if chosen, he should be obeyed and given a chance to serve the people until that people dispossesses him for another.

It is very evil, very shameful and savage in these enlightened days of education and science for America to be charged with killing her rulers and great men of wisdom and science without due process of law.

There is no justice for us, the so-called Negroes, in a government whose citizens are free to kill until satisfied and then turn upon their rulers and slay them. What chance have we under the rule of such people? We live under the very shadow of death all the day long.

The assassinated President Abraham Lincoln, by John W. Booth in Washington, D.C., April 14, 1865 — who died April 15, 1865 — was successful in freeing our parents from servitude slavery; to weaken the slave master's strength against the Federal Government. For this he paid with his life.

President James A. Garfield, assassinated by

117

Charles J. Guiteau, July 2, 1881, in Washington, D.C. and died September 19, 1881. President William McKinley, shot September 6, 1901, in Buffalo, New York, by Leon Czolgosy, and died September 14, 1901.

President John F. Kennedy, assassinated November 22, 1963, in Dallas, Texas, by the accused assassin Lee Harvey Oswald, and died minutes later. All four of these presidents were known to have spoken and acted sympathetically towards the so-called Negroes, and they paid with their lives for doing so.

There are others who had attempts made upon their lives. Mr. Huey P. Long, U.S. Senator of Louisiana, was shot September 18, 1935, in Baton Rouge, Louisiana, by Dr. Carl A. Weiss, and died September 19, 1935. Mr. Long preached "share the wealth." And for this he paid with his life.

There is no justice for the poor, the so-called Negroes in America as long as they are subjects under the American flag. A great attempt is now being made on the poor, lost found, so called Negroes to deceive them by making false friendship, and the passage of Civil Rights bills, and forcing themselves to accept the lost-found (so-called Negroes) into their social equality.

This is only a trap for us. To accept it will make us enemies of God and our Black people of Africa and Asia who are our true friends. It would be totally ignorant on our part to be swept away to our doom by accepting these maelstrom promises of social equality temptations. Our ignorant masses cannot be trusted under the charms (temptation) of un-alike. But in the end you will regret your actions.

If America wants to offer us a better side of her,

why not offer something of permanent good, such as a portion of the country (a few states) for our ever-increasing population? Will the white man fool himself in continuously making promises to us that he knows he cannot fulfill? He has his own problems of u n e m p l o y m e n t, with the e v e r-i n c r e a s i n g unemployed of his own kind fleeing from Asia and Africa, plus the loss of foreign trade.

Can we hope for him to care for us and our children forever? No! We need a place on this earth that we can call our own, and go to work and produce our own needs; and this will provide us with employment for our unemployed. Let no man deceive you; we are face to face with a change of worlds.

CHAPTER 29

Fall and Rise of Nations

The title of this chapter is taken from the 13th Chapter of the Holy Qur'an entitled "The Thunder."

We have past histories that teach us of the fall and rise of many nations. However, in this day — after this destruction of the nations, there will be no rise of these destroyed nations because Allah (God) Who came in the Person of Master Fard Muhammad to Whom praises are due forever, will destroy those who cause evil to spread far and wide. He will destroy those who love to make war on others, as it is written, Ps. 68:30.

During the whole time of the mischief-maker (devil)- six thousand years on our planet—there has been one war right after another. There has never been any peace among them. You cannot live with them in peace. Peace was never in the nature of the white race.

The white race was made to destroy the peace from the earth and they have just about destroyed the peace from the earth. The Bible, Isaiah, as it is written, "The people know not the way of peace."

Why should peace - lovers want a world to live in where there is no peace? If peace can be established, the nations want peace, but they cannot have peace until the power of the peace-breaker has been broken.

America is angry over the possible freedom of her Black once - slave to go for himself and to set up self - independence. America is angry and does not want the Black slave to seek some other nations to help him.

There are other nations whose populations run into hundreds of millions of people and these hundreds of millions of people of other nations have sympathy for the Black man in America. They hope to help the Black man in America to be free to go for self, while white America is working with all of her might in order to prevent the nations from giving any aid to the Black Man in America.

If other nations give Black man in America any aid, white America wants to hinder us.

A people who are that wicked against the Black slave, whom they have had for four hundred years — Allah (God) should not have any pity on His destruction of them — nor should the nations of earth pity white America, because white America is wicked beyond your and my imagination.

White America turned the world into evil, filth and indecency. You cannot go out into the streets accompained by your decent families without your being made ashamed of the work of the white man. He has made it lawful for people to go nude if they want to do so.

It is a dangerous world for a person who loves to live in peace and who desires to keep his own property as well as his life—it is a dangerous world.

The rise of ancient Babylon — with her persecution of the righteous among her and with her hatred of the Jews and their religion — Babylon was brought to naught. Is America better than ancient Babylon? No!

The people of Noah committed the same evil and the same unsightly filth that is going on here in America, today. But, the evil and filth of the present day America, is being committed on a larger scale than that committed in the day of Noah. The people of Noah were drowned and destroyed.

So it was with the people of Lot. In Sodom and Gomorrah wickedness and filth had become the order of the day. Those wicked people were removed from our planet earth. Is America any better? No! America is worse than that ancient people.

White America sees that we, the Islamic believers, the Muslims, want to do something for self and our Black kind. But white America opposes us to a degree that she destroys our cattle, our farm instruments and our machinery.

White America wants to destroy our lives. White America is planning to destroy our lives, but Allah (God) too is planning, and Allah (God) is the Best of the planners. The fall and rise of nations!

The fall and rise of nations! The quickest way for America to hasten her fall is to try and to mistreat and to do evil to me and to my followers. The quickest way for America to receive her approaching hour (doom) is for America to always to try to find some way to block the success of Allah (God) in guiding me and those who are following me.

America! As soon as white America learned that we are trying to purchase wholesale quantities of low - priced merchandise from Japan for the benefit of all of my Black people in America— America goes in to make it hard for me and my followers to purchase and to receive anything from outside of America at a lower price than we pay to America. This is evil on the part of America.

America will have to learn us! America will have to learn that we the Black people in America are the brothers of the Black people, the Brown people and the Yellow people.

We have many Muslims in these lands and to try to interfere with the success of the Muslims in America, which is coming from Allah (God) Himself — Allah (God) will continue to confuse America; and she will have the loss of her victory in any land and among any people on earth. Fall and rise of nations!

CHAPTER 30

She Had Become The Habitation of Devils (Rev. 18:2)

This is America, the glory of the world in wealth, sport and play, with her merchants ships ploughing the high seas carrying her costly merchandise throughout the population of the nations of the earth. (Bible, Rev. 18:19).

The ships of America can be seen everywhere... in every port of the nations of earth. Her great navy is built to command the high seas. Her decks are mounted with great bristling rifle-barrelled guns. The decks of her ships are covered with planes with which to carry deadly bomb-shells to pour on other nations who dare now to reject her entrance into their waters. The writer, (John), foresaw America threatening and daring the nations to disobey her order to allow her entrance. America's navy planes fly high in the air with their deadly bombs held ready to drop on the towns and cities of other nations who dare to attack her.

The sky over America is shadowed with thousands of planes, but yet the grievous destruction awaits America. America sends planes flying out of her country and shoots herself out into space by means of the most modern rockets designed for space - travel!

At home, America's country is as the prophet foresaw and prophesied of it; America is covered with planes and her army is standing ready to stop inside rebellion. The prophet who foresaw all of this readiness and preparation for the world showdown of military might, says, "Woe to the land shadowing with wings..." (Bible Is. 18:1).

America takes a look around the dead piece of our earth... the moon. She wants to see if they can do her harm. America takes a look at Venus and Mars to see if there are signs of any gods on these planets who are capable of warring with her. America boasts of her ability to kill the civilization of earth three times over and have an army left to attack anywhere else that an enemy may rise up against her.

Nebuchadnezzar and Belshazzar, who were the world rulers of their day and time, made great boasts. Pharaoh also made great mock of Allah (Jehovah) and His power to attack Pharaoh. In the Holy Qur'an, Pharaoh said to Moses concerning Allah, The Lord of the Worlds, Chap. 20:49: "Who is your Lord, O Moses?" Pharaoh said to his slave, Moses, in words to say, "You take another God besides me? Holy Qur'an, Ch. 20:71,"... "So I (Pharaoh) shall cut off your hands and feet on opposite sides..." But Israel took another God Allah (Jehovah) besides Pharaoh and they did not lose their hands and feet on opposite sides.

The people cry about death and destruction playing havoc over America, but they never cry about the evil that they are committing and which is the cause of this destruction coming into her borders bringing floods, rain, ice, hail and earthquakes daily and nightly somewhere on the surface of the land of America.

The Bible refers to America by the name, Babylon, and teaches us, Rev. 18:2, "...Babylon the great is fallen, is fallen, and is become the habitation of devils, and the hole of every foul spirit, and a cage

125

of every unclean and hateful bird." This is true, for America has accepted immigrants of the most evil and lewd character from Europe. America has filled her country with evil and indecency and there is no good in the works of America. America hates the doers of good and seeks to destroy them. This is the cause of the fall of America.

You can bear witness to the deadly storms and twisters that are striking America in the areas where some of you live. Can you not see that Allah (God) is after you for the evil done to His people (Black man).

The rich, the wealthy and powerful rulers of America, from the mayors of cities, the police commissioners up to the President work to oppose the Black once-slave's return to his own. All of this hastens their doom, as the Bible, Ps. 2:4, teaches us, "He that sitteth in the heavens shall laugh: the Lord shall have them in derision."

Allah (God) laughs at their struggle to bring to a naught His aims and purpose of freedom, justice and equality to His Black people. Allah (God) has them (heads of America) in derision and confusion to the limit of their wits. In another place, the Bible teaches us, that He (Allah) will turn them backward. (Is. 44:25)

Evil and filth are the god and worship of America. Never has a people on the face of the earth become so bold in their evil practices. Never before America has there been a nation on the face of the earth where scores of murders take place daily and nightly. In one large metropolitan city of America, the death rate is terrific...children kill children...male is against male and female is against female, destroying each other.

The woman has no shyness. American designers and manufacturers dress the woman up in about one third of a dress and turn her out partially nude before the public. You would not expect to witness this in a country that preaches Christ Jesus and has churches dotting, here and there, throughout the land. You can hardly walk two or three blocks in a city without walking into the door of a church. The Christians profess to be the most truly righteous people in the country. All night long their voices are heard on the air preaching Jesus Christ, the prophet who lived two thousand years ago. He is dead and cannot hear the prayers of anyone, not even his own. The Christian preachers try to fool you by telling you that if you pray to the prophet Jesus that he will hear you. This is false. He cannot hear you. If it were true, why cannot they get him to hear them when they call for peace anywhere?

Their doctrine is used to deceive the Black man, so that he will stay on his knees praying to something from which he will never get an answer. He will never get any answer from a dead prophet.

What kind of little girl can we expect from a mother who is walking around one-half naked and is displaying herself to the world, dressed in such a dress that no animal would wear? There is more shyness displayed in animals than there is in the so-called Christian American dressed in a mini-dress.

The Black woman should be too proud of herself to disgrace herself in the same manner as her white slave-mistress. The Black man should be sent to prison for being such a fool as to allow his wife and daughter to go out and show their nude selves to the public.

Nudity originated from the white race. Now they want to say to the world that "I am the guide." The guide to what? The Holy Qur'an says that they lead you to nothing but filth and evil. The Bible is referring to the people of America when it is referring to the people of Sodom and Gomorrah. Allah (God) destroyed them when he saw that it was good to do so. (Gen. 19:13). As it was with Sodom and Gomorrah, so it will be with America.

CHAPTER 31

"Mystery Babylon, The Great"

According to the English interpretation, the word "mystery" means unknown uncertain, obscure, concealed, a secret, kept to oneself, between you and me, locked up, something that has not been or cannot be explained. In theology it is a supposed truth of fact of great religious import which is beyond human comprehension. In the time of the translation of the Bible into English, some or all of the scholars were either without spiritual understanding or downright crooks who sought to hide that truth in the Book that they thought would reveal to the world their untrue selves. The "Mystery Babylon" had not come into existence.

In ancient times Babylon, under the Kings Nebuchadnezzar and Belshazzar, was the great city of idol worship and evil. She was the Queen of Evil — rich and well fortified. But this "Mystery Babylon" must refer to a future city or people. No city or people answers the description better than the cities and people of America. This "Mystery Babylon" just could not be the ancient Babylon as we know her history.

You must remember that I am interested in bringing the truth to my people as clear as sunshine. So be not distrubed in seeing and hearing it the clear and simple way; for my people are the blind, deaf and dumb of the nations of the earth. They must be taught the truth by one who knows it. I am he who knows the truth, and I have been missioned from the Lord of the Worlds to tell the truth, whether it is to your liking or disliking.

America (and her future) was not known in those days when the Bible was being translated into the English language. Not until 1611 did the translators bring into existence what is known as the King James Authorized Version. According to history, there were several attempts made before to get the Bible to the people in the English language, but they were met with opposition.

America was discovered in 1492. These first translations of the Bible were far more near the truth than these later translations. The so-called Negro slaves were not given the King James Version to read until it was over three hundred years old. The white slave masters were not interested in "educated religious Negroes" (and are not toay). The so-called Negroes now must understand that which was hidden from them by their slavemasters.

The "Mystery Babylon, the Great" is none other than America. This "Mystery Babylon" is full of riches, hatred, filth, fornication, adultery, drunkenness, murder of the innocent and idol worship. "Mystery Babylon" is full of names of blasphemy. America is full of various religious faiths of the most ignorant kind. She was once the greatest slave buyer and seller. She has the greatest merchant marine service, the world's greatest export shippers in the merchandise of wheat, beasts, sheep, horses, chariots, gold, silver, iron, brass, wood, slaves, fine flour, corn and many others.

You must know that all of the Revelation, or at least 90 per cent, is directed to America. The seventeenth and eighteenth chapters should open the so-called Negroes' eyes to the white race and white Christianity. There is no hereafter for the white race. Some few who are in Asia will stick around for a while.

CHAPTER 32

Babylon Could Have Been Saved, But She Was Not

America seems to be the answer to many of the Bible's and the Holy Qur'an's prophecies. It is mentioned in Jeremiah (51:9) that ancient Babylon could have been healed but was not, for her wickedness was such that she was neither healed nor forgiven.

The charges against ancient Babylon, according to her history, were that she persecuted and imprisoned the Jews. She brought them into captivity from Jerusalem after the taking of Jerusalem by Nebuchadnezzar.

Nebuchadnezzar was also punished for his part in the enslavement, according to the ancient history of Babylon. King Nebuchadnezzar had among the Jews whom he held in captivity, Daniel, a prophet of Israel. The King did not love Daniel and his prophethood, but he was able to get Allah's prophecy of the destruction of Babylon from Daniel. But remember, he still held Daniel as a slave and a prisoner with the other common Jews.

Under King Belshazzar, Daniel was still alive and was used for the revealing of God's aims and purposes against Babylon.

After studying the history of the destruction of ancient Babylon under these two kings, we have a very good graphic picture pointing to a future people and country. The words, ''We would have healed Babylon, but she is not healed'' do not say why she was not healed. Was there a possible chance for the

131

Babylonians being forgiven because of the evils done to the Jews, the sacking of Jerusalem, the destruction of their temple, and the bringing out from her temples sacred vessels to be used for sport under Belshazzar's reign? Could this crime of the Babylonians be forgiven? And if not forgiven, what does this teach us?

Is not the history of ancient Babylon's unforgiven evils a sign that a future enslavement of God's people (the American so-called Negro) will not be forgiven? Yet, there may be a chance, as Babylon had, but they will not do that which God desires them to do so that He may pardon them and forgive them and prolong their time.

The Revelations of John's prophecies were that they repented not of their evil deeds but blasphemed the very name of God (Rev. 16:9.) Therefore, when a man is guilty of a great evil done against the cause of God and His people, he cannot be forgiven unless he seeks forgiveness himself.

We see this in the working of the fall of America today. I say fall, for most surely this is the divine fall of America., as it was of ancient Babylon for its evils done to the Jews.

Even to this late date, America does not want to repent of her evil done to her Black slaves. I have given her a right chance, but she does not want to do justice by her free slaves to get an extension of time from Allah. She should free the slaves indeed. The ignorant ones who want to stay with her just because they are too lazy to accept their own responsibilities, or too much in love with the unalike white people who have attracted them to such an extent that they have become a charm — want to remain with this white master even if they are just given food and shelter—

132

this type of people is not wanted by any nation. No nation wants slaves on the basis of taking the responsibility to care for them when they can care for themselves.

The American Black once slave for four hundred years had now become a free proud slave, and a lover of the children of the once slave-masters.

The refusal of white America to do something about justice for her so-called free slaves is bringing her into the same type of judgment that God brought upon ancient Babylon.

Jeremiah (51:45) mentions a warning to the people of God to flee out of Babylon. Could this be referring to the captive Jews in ancient Babylon? If God called the ancient Jews His people, it was for a sign of a future people that He would choose to call His people (The American so-called Negro).

The Black people of America today are called His chosen people by God Himself, chosen by Him to build a new government based upon truth, freedom, justice and equality. This type of government is to live forever and never to be removed from the people, according to Daniel's prophecy of a kingdom of God set up in the last days — the government of which will not be left to the people. God Himself will be the head and the ruler.

In ancient Babylon's history, the enslaved Jews were ordered to flee out of her midst and be delivered, every man his soul from the fierce anger of the Lord, Jeremiah (51:45.)

The last book of the Bible, the Revelations of John (18:4) makes this a little clearer. Both prophecies are similar but the one in Revelations is warning a people to flee out of Babylon so that they..."Be not partakers of her sins," of Babylon and receive not of her plagues."

This showed that God was going to plague Babylon; and that His people should not suffer the divine plagues sent upon Babylon. They are ordered to flee out of her. (Jeremiah 51:45.) This is a future prophecy of a future Babylon similar to the ancient Babylon under the rule of Nebuchadnezzar. The history of these two kings of ancient Babylon teaches us that they held slaves who were trying to serve the right God.

The coming of Allah in the Person of Master coming of Allah in the Person of Master Fard Muhammad, to Whom praises are due forever, was for the deliverance of the lost-and-found people (Black) from a four-hundred year-old enemy who has never shown them anything but evil, murder and death. Being very angry, as it was written of Him and as I know it to be the truth, He desires nothing more than freedom, justice, and equality for us, the once lost and now found Black members of our nation, the original Black nation of the earth.

America now is at war with God through God's people (the so-called Negro.) The confusion and the plagues of the country with disasters, one after another, is divine retaliation against white America's evil doings and intentions, against her once-slaves and her false friendship, which has her opening her homes to integrate the people of God with them who by nature are different or foreign. The white man has poisoned our people's minds so thoroughly that they fight against their own God and salvation to gain the favor of their own enemies.

The call of Islam, the true religion of God to us, the once-slaves of America, is the same call telling us to flee out of the American way of life so that our lives may be saved from the divine destruction of a non-repentant enemy (Jeremiah 51:45.)

Divine plagues and foreign wars are now destroying the American standards of life and money. Her deceitful, filthy temptations, now being displayed before her once-slaves in the world, are designed to make the once-slave an enemy of his God and of his own salvation; and are designed to make them take part with them against the aim and purpose of Allah, which is to set the so-called Negro in heaven while he lives.

A prophecy relating to America is mentioned in Isaiah (47:1) as a "virgin daughter" of ancient Babylon's history. As we all know, America is the last, the greatest and the richest remaining power of the white nations. But now she is falling and the prophet Isaiah says, "Come and sit down in the dust," humble yourself, for you are no more called delicate.

The filthy display by white American Christians, walking around half nude, sitting before their pastors in their churches with dresses halfway up their thighs for the pastors to stare at their nude forms goes on. The pastor should actually be standing at the door telling such disgracefully dressed people that he preaches the word of God and that God warns us to be clean, both internally and externally, and that we should not tempt the nation to do evil and filth. But he opens his church doors and is happy to have them in rows sitting before his eyes, knowing that this is against the teaching of God; turning his house of God into the worship of filth and evil.

Can the church survive? Can Christianity survive these days of divine judgment against America?

The Revelation reads, in a prophecy relating to America, that she had in her a "hole for every foul spirit, and a cage of every unclean and hateful bird" (Revelation 18:2.) All hateful people have a haven in America. Though the scientists and scholars of the religion of Christianity know these words to be true, they desire yet to see the already - made blind, deaf and dumb so-called Negro go to his doom with them; and since they are by nature evil, they tempt them. The Holy Qur'an teaches that they only lead you to filth and evil. This is perfectly manifested today in America among its people ruled by the white man. The very conscience of an individual knows that these evils we see today are not accepted by God.

The desire to marry and integrate among people whom God has made to be His and our enemies is beyond one's imagination.

Jeremiah (51:46) prophesies violence in the midst of Babylon (a future Babylon) and "ruler against ruler." Is not this true of the American government and people today? "Her whole land (people) shall be confounded" (Jeremiah 51:47.) Is not this true of the American government and people today? They are fast becoming confounded "And all her slain shall fall in the midst of her" Jeremiah 5l:47 .) Every hour in the day and night people are being murdered and killed in America throughout her cities and highways.

136

Murdering and killing is the order of the day in America.

The Bible mentions that God used a destroying wind (Jeremiah 51:1) against those who opposed His purpose and aims. Is it not true that day and night somewhere in America there are destructive tornadoes and storms destroying the property and lives of Americans?

Go to sleep to the reality of the judgment of America, a repetition of ancient Babylon's judgment, if you like to be caught in the snare. As God has said, He laid a snare for ancient Babylon (Jeremiah 50:24) and ancient Babylon was taken in that snare.

So it is in America. Long before America ever thought that she should repent of her evil done to her slaves or reject repentance, God hath set the snare to catch her. America is now in the same snare that God set for ancient Babylon. Will America repent that she should be healed or will she ignore it?

CHAPTER 33

Modern Babylon is falling

We say "modern" when we refer to something comparing it to the past. This name "Babylon" begins in Genesis 10:10 (Bible). In Gen. 10:10 it is spelled "B-a-b-e-l." But the same name seems to have changed itself into the name Babylon as we come to the most late-day history of this name.

Babel (Babylon)—According to the history of Babylon throughout the Bible, Babylon is referred to as something prophesied as having a failure upon her progress and rise.

In Psalms 137:18, David prophesies that Babylon was made to be destroyed. We know of nothing other than the devil and his works that was actually made to be destroyed spiritually.

The devil was not made to exist forever. This is verified by both the Bible and the Holy Qur'an and by all writers and teachers of scripture. So, here, Babylon seems to refer not only to some town or city, but it also seems to refer to a race or a nation of people.

Ancient Babylon, as is known by all of us, was a city under the reign of Nebuchadnezzar and Belshazzar. The fall of Babylon was final. Babylon was never to be rebuilt after her fall. And Babylon was never rebuilt.

This points to the same prophecy of the devil and his kingdom in the Revelation of John (Bible)—that satan and his kingdom would be burnt up and it would never rise again.

In the Epistles of Paul there is a prophecy of the devil and his kingdom 'that the devil was made for fuel for the fire." The Holy Qur'an refers to this prophecy in these words: "Fuel of hell is men and stones."

So the "fuel of hell is men and stones"—we do not know why stones are put there with men-it could be referring to the hardness of the stone and to the hardness of the heart and the hardness of the wicked against truth and righteousness.

In the book of Revelation (Bible), it is prophesied here that an angel heralded a warning to the people that Babylon is falling. He then tells why Babylon fell. Babylon fell because she... "is become the habitation of devils, and the hole of every foul spirit, and a cage of every unclean and hateful bird." The "foul spirit" here is used to tell us that the people of Babylon were filthy.

The term, "a cage"— this tells us that her cities and her country became a cage for people of filth. The Bible teaches us that the God referred to the people of Sodom and Gomorrah as being people whose doing and work was such that it came up and stunk in His nostrils. (But I think that if the God would get a good smell of this modern wicked filth here He would think the smell of Babylon in His nostrils was like the smell of a flower compared to the wickedness of today.)

Babylon is used as an example for some distant people or their history. According to the prophets, this name Babylon is something that begins in Genesis and ends in Revelation. It is found throughout the entire Bible; therefore, we must not look at it as one personal part. We must not look at it as spelling out to us the ancient only.

In Jeremiah, (Bible) we see a daughter of ancient Babylon. He calls the people "the daughters of

139

ancient Babylon." These people are not the old parents, but they are the daughters from those parents.

The daughter of ancient Babylon refers to a more late and modern civilization whose people give themselves over to the practice of the same evil that the people of Ancient Babylon practiced. But, the modern people were more capable of improving on the practices of the people of ancient Babylon. Therefore,he calls this modern people "the daughters of ancient Babylon."

Isaiah (Bible Is. 47:1) asks this people, the daughter of Babylon, "Come down, and sit in the dust, O virgin daughter of Babylon,sit on the ground: there is no throne...for thou shalt no more be called tender and delicate."

The daughters of Babylon seem to have been a very rich people and they had fallen from a state of great wealth. Isaiah used Babylon as a pretty girl whose lovers used to be plentiful because of her wealth and attractiveness; now she has become ill-looking and has no more attraction upon the people. So he said, sit down in the dust, you are no more respected and attractive to the people.

The prophet Jeremiah warned ancient Babylon that she had a daughter coming. This daughter meets the fate destined for Babylon: she was made to be taken.

Satan was made to be taken and destroyed. Why? Because she had become a place where evil was practiced. She was like a bird that goes out and associates with birds other than her own kind, and then she becomes a hateful bird—she is hated by the other birds.

Babylon fills herself up with people of that sort. The U.S.A. came into the Western Hemisphere and chased and all but annihilated the Indians. But America invited every one of the poor class who wanted to come from Europe to make themselves at home here in America, the Indians' country.

All of the poor and evil citizens of Europe, America welcomed them. She invited every race of the earth to come and join in with her in a free country where evil and filth are openly practiced without hindrance.

America has done just this. She has filled up her country with all evil people. America did not allow Islam, nor a preacher of Islam, to come into her country; America did not want a good religion taught. America made a religion that she could rule and control herself. She made it attractive to the eyes and ears of those who see and hear it by teaching them basically that there were three Gods instead of teaching them the teachings of Moses and the prophets—the teaching of one God.

America makes it possible in her God-Head that if one of them does not like you, you may plead to another and if one does not let you by, one of the three will. This is contrary to the very law of nature. It is contrary to America's own mathematical language. In mathematics it is not possible to put three (3) into one (1).

So, America, having this religion, contrary to the truth, today the Author of Truth is condemning her (America). America is nothing but a foul and evil place to live. She has no respect for her own self nor for anyone else. She will disrobe in the public and go nudist. America even has nudist colonies wherein if you desire to go nude you can do so if the public does not want you.

In the Bible, Rev. 18:4,5 in the Revelation of John, a people are warned to flee out of her. Here, we get the name Babylon to become a modern day people. The voice of an angel warns the people of a certain class to fly out of Babylon. "...Come out of her, my people, that ye be not partakers of her sins, and that ye receive not of her plagues. For her sins have reached unto heaven, and God hath remembered her iniquities" (as being an evil people). So the angel notifies us saying, "Babylon the great is fallen." Today, we see this same thing.

There is no people to be warned to come out of another people that answers to the description of this warning so clearly as the so-called Negro in America of lost-found people of our own Black kind does.

Here, the so-called Negro is warned to fly out of her and not to be partakers of her judgment—her torment. The angel says, so much evil has she done to thee Rev. 18:6, "Reward her even as she rewarded you, and double unto her double according to her works: in the cup which she hath filled fill to her double."

Allah (God) in the Person of Master Fard Muhammad, to Whom praises are due forever, said to me that there is nothing that you can do to her in the way of evil that could match the evil that she has already done to us.

This is why the Revelator calls the people of modern Babylon "beasts," for they live the kind of life of wild beasts. They have no mercy for themselves or for anyone else. They are made

142

merciless although there are a few who will believe and escape the doom of her brothers. This is their reward just by faith.

But the Black man is created by the Creator, by nature, and he was made blind, deaf and dumb by his kidnapping lord and master, the white slave-master. I do not think that you could overlook the most positive truth here, in this article, that we are now living in the call of angel to us, to come out of her. The "her" here means the wicked world of the devil.

Since we the Black people were kidnapped and forced into this world (of the white race) we must be forced out of this world. It is not that you my people will accept by just having the freedom to accept of your own choice. No. You will have to be punished, divinely beaten and destroyed until you accept Master Fard Muhammad, to Whom praises are Due forever, as your God and Saviour, as I and thousands of my followers are doing.

Do not think that the 144,000 prophesied of, are the only ones who will be saved. The 144,000 refers to the first converts—"the first ripe fruits to God and His Messenger, the first ripe fruits of God and the Lamb."

Another prophecy warns us that "Babylon is falling never to rise again." In this warning it teaches you that the country and people of modern Babylon will become like the people and city of ancient Babylon that was destroyed and has not risen up a people or a city since its destruction.

I warn you my Black brother and Black sister that unless you believe in Almighty God Allah, Master Fard Muhammad, as I do and receive the name of the holy and perfect God you will never see the hereafter.

The Bible warns you and me that on the final destruction of the wicked, Allah (God) will say to the angel that He has to usher in the judgment to bring His people to Him everyone that is called by His name. For He gives His people His name so that He may save them. So that they may be the servant of Allah (God) as they were the servant of the white slave-master.

As long as you are in the name of the white slave-master, you belong to the white slave-master. And regardless to what you believe and regardless to how mighty you think that you are, you will not be accepted by the Black people and the God of our Black people if you have the name of white people and if you are in the religion called Christianity.

The fall of America is now going on! She is falling! The cause of her fall is universally known, as it was with ancient Babylon. The fall of ancient Babylon was known. The great prophet Daniel, the mouth-speak of God, was in her midst; and his people (the Jews) were enslaved.

In ancient Babylon, according to history, during the reign of Nebuchadnezzar and Belshazzar, the Jews suffered under the ruthless law of these two kings against the Jewish God, religion, and people. These two rulers of ancient Babylon disrespected everything regarding the sacred religion and worship of Jehovah by the Jews.

They took Jerusalem and captured the nobles of Israel. They raided and sacked the city and the Jews' house of worship. They made mockery and shambles of all that stood for Jehovah and the Jews.

They made mockery of the prophets and the sacred vessels that God had King Solomon make and put in the house of worship of the Jews so that they should be sacred.

Nebuchadnezzar and his nephew (or grandson, according to some historians) Belshazzar gave the Jews no honor and no respect whatsoever. Under both of their reigns, God made an example of them to serve as an example of a future people's opposition and disrespect of God and His people.

Master Fard Muhammad, Who is Allah in Person, wants to make it clear that He has chosen the American so-called Negroes to be His people. The truth that He gives to them and they, themselves, are sacred before His eyes and the world of the righteous. Showing disrespect to God and His people is inviting the punishment and doom of God.

A careful observer or seeker of truth of the time and history being made in these times can easily see how well the history of ancient Babylon, its rulers and its people fits in with the histories of the rulers and peoples of America and England.

America's enslavement of the so-called Negro and England's enslavement of people fit so completely with the history of ancient Babylon that it cannot be denied that the ancient history of the Babylonian empire and people was prototypal of America.

America wants everyone to believe she is right in her wicked dealings with the people of earth. With her might of arms commanding the high seas and the land around the globe, she wishes everyone to think she is right in building up arms and forts in foreign countries and on their shores a bristling, deadly navy with guns trained on foreign peoples' towns and cities, as a dare without any cause. This only shows her pride and

145

daring aggressive acts against people who would like to be at peace.

She has her feet standing on twenty or thirty million Black people, brought out of their native land and people — from their God and their religion — by her fathers and have forced them to remain under her feet of power for the past four-hundred years. She deprived them of the knowledge of self, the white race, their own people and their religion.

For three hundred years she did not allow them to worship any religion at all — not even her own religion of Christianity. She robbed them of their divine rights.

Now with her great show of temptation put before the same slaves and the world at large, she should not be surprised to see and feel the hand of God writing her doom on the wall of her government.

CHAPTER 34

The Judgment of America

The great dreadful days of the Lord have now come to America — the land and people who worship evil and indecency. Robbery, murder, rape, famine and deceit are the order of the day in America.

If there is anything like a God of Righteousness — if there is anything like a God of Truth — should not He raise himself up and take His place and put an end to such evil as is now going on in America?

People cannot walk the streets of America today without subjecting themselves to robbery, murder or rape. America is a wicked land...everyone is against the other.

Righteousness, justice and freedom are despised and fought against regardless to the clear knowledge of God's hourly punishment and destruction of America by His divine plague of storms. But this is as it is written of America in the Book of Revelations, in the Bible... 'they continue their evil way and did blaspheme the God Who has power over the plagues. They hated the name of Allah, the Great Mahdi..they hated the name of His Messenger..but nevertheless that does not stop the judgment and the destruction of America.

Look at the wicked devils in Alabama. They are against us while we are trying to be at peace with them, but there is no peace in them. We have done nothing to them. They are against us just because of the idea that we are Muslims and Black people.

The white man has had his way of ruling the Black people for so long that he thinks that he still has the power to do so while in reality the white man has come to the end of his time of power to rule the Black people.

Regardless to Allah's (God's) Retaliation to the white man for his evil acts done to the Black man, the white man still keeps inviting the retaliation of Allah (God). The white man must remember that he cannot win today over Allah (God) and His Servant, for He has power over the fraction of an atom.

The judgment of America. Judgment has come to you America. Woe to you who seek to fight against Allah (God) and against His aim and purpose. Woe to you America. Allah (God) has made you blind to His judgment and therefore you are committing suicide. He has made you blind on purpose...to give you the full dose of His wrath, for when a man does not know the danger of fire, then he can fall headlong into it.

America has mistreated the Black man for four hundred years and she does not think that there is ever a God Who will accept her Black slave and return on her head the injustice done to her Black slave.

This is the day and time in which America could benefit from what Allah (God) has revealed to me and from the work that I am doing among my Black people...turning them from doing evil into righteousness. As it is written in the Bible, "Babylon could have been healed;" and there was a possible chance for her healing, if she had not gone to the extreme by making fun of the God of the Jews and their temple in Jerusalem and belittling the power of the God of the Jews, to retaliate.

The Bible prophesies of the plagues that would come upon America — and these plagues are falling on America now, and yet she will not repent. For America continues to kill and deprive the Black once slave of righteousness and justice. Even though the Black slave wants to go from America, she wants to hold on to him and America does not want to let her Black once - slave go. America holds the Black once - slave for a prey.

Woe to America. Her day has arrived. She would not heed the warning. I begged her to let us be separated from her on a little territory and a state to ourselves and to let us be responsible for our own survival, only to get out from under her injustice; but she refused. So it was with Pharaoh in the time of Moses. God went down to Egypt to make Israel and her enemies, the Egyptians, an example for a future people so that this may serve as a sign of what we see going on in America today.

The four (4) Great Judgments that Allah (God) promises to destroy America with are now coming upon her...hail, snow, drought, earthquake. Allah (God) has reserved His treasures of snow and ice to be used against the wicked country America in the day of battle and war. These are some of Allah's (God's) weapons, the storms that we see going on.

The white man of America is not blind and ignorant. He has known these prophecies of his doom for a long time before we knew it, for the white man translated the Bible and he knows what he put in his translation of that which was written in the Bible.

The judgment of America. All love and respect of the wicked has gone from them. They do not love each other nor respect each other. They have pulled off their clothes and disgraced themselves. This is also a plague. You see some of the white people rehearsing the cave days of their fathers, and they are not ashamed to do so. They come out with long, straggly hair as their fathers did in the days of the cave. This is Allah (God) forcing the white man to bear Him Witness that they were really once the cave man. Yet a few foolish, unlearned Black People follow the white man. It is a shame to pull off their clothes and grow hair down their back and over their face. By misleading the Black man into following the way of the white man's cave days, the white man is again telling the world how he has deceived the Black man and is now making the Black man manifest that he is too weak to seek his own.

For nearly forty years I have been preaching to the Black man in America that we should accept our own; and instead of the Black man going to the decent side of his own, he goes back seeking traditional Africa, and the way they did in jungle life and the way you see in some uncivilized parts of Africa today. They are not using barber's tools, shears, and razors to keep themselves looking dignified as a civilized people should look. The Black man in America accepts the jungle life, thinking that they would get the love of Black Africa. Black brother and Black sister, wearing savage dress and hair-styles will not get you the love of Africa. The dignified people of Africa are either Muslim or educated Christians. But Africa today does not want Christianity. Do not think that you will get a home in Africa after this war if you are Christian. To get a home in Africa after the war, you will have to be Muslim.

The Judgment of America. She is made manifest.

As it is written in the Bible, (Revelation, "She is a cage of every unclean and hateful bird" (every unclean and hateful human being).

America, America your day has come for the evil done to your Black Slave. America you cannot repay that evil with another evil of trying to tempt the Black slave by offering them your white women. That does not help you in this day, but it does condemn you as being a double - crosser...that you will even offer your Black once-slave your girls and women to do with them as they please, if they will just follow you.

The judgment of America. "Babylon could have been healed but she was not healed."

America is just beginning to experience sorrow, mourning, grief and distrust from the anger of God and man.

According to both the Holy Qur'an and the Bible, there will be plenty more of the same. In these two books, one can easily find everything foretold that is happening today. The time will grow so troublesome that (according to the Holy Qur'an) children will become gray headed, and (according to the Bible) great heart failure will become a disease upon the people, who have the anger of God (the American people).

The fourth beast in the Revelations of John in the Bible—and of which Daniel describes as a very dreadful and well armed beast, whose workings are that of death upon the weak—refers to America. She has no respect for the poor and the unfortunate.

Daniel's description of the ribs between the teeth of the beast is in reference to this ill-treatment, subjection, and ruthless behavior by the devil to our people.

This America ladens the poor with heavy sentences—long prison terms—and refuses to let the prisoners go free. This is due to her heartlessness and lack of compassion for the Black man of America.

This beast (white man) lies in wait around the Black man's homes and prowls the streets at night in wait for an excuse to wreak his ruthlessness on his poor prey (the Black man). If the Black man raises a hand to protect and defend himself, he is shot dead, and is unable to defend himself against false charges.

This beast keeps our people in sorrow and unhappiness by depriving them of equal opportunities. The Black man's wages are calculated by white wicked accountants, preventing the so-called Negro from saving by skyrocketing (in the view of the poor) the prices of the necessities of life.

This white beast prosecutes, imprisons and kills those who preach freedom and justice for the poor so-called Negroes. The white man does not want the so-called Negroes to leave America; but she will not divide the spoils of America (the country which she has taken by the force of arms and killing its aboriginal owners, the Indians) with them.

This beast sets up evil and indecency to be idolized as a God. She disguises good for evil and she covers the earth with filth, making it fascinating so that men will bow down and worship evil for good. She sets brother against brother for her joy; then she kills both of them.

Woe to America, the murderer and deceiver of the people. The God of Justice and Truth has pronounced a judgment against thee—and by no means will you escape. You have made mockery of Him, God, and His people and His word, the truth.

You have been judged and found wanting to the so-called American Negroes, the lost and now found members of the aboriginal Black nation of the earth.

Come, unite with Allah, and me. Go to your own. You won't have to go anywhere if you only will unite with your own. Heaven awaits you wherever you may be.

CHAPTER 35

America Surrounded with The Judgment of Allah

The four great judgments that Almighty Allah (God) is bringing upon America are rain, hail, snow and earthquakes. We see them now covering all sides of America, as the Holy Qur'an prophesies, curtailing her on all her sides. And these judgments would push the people into the center of the country, and there they would realize that it is Allah (God) Who is bringing them and their country to a naught.

Job, in the Bible, prophesied that Allah (God) has the snow and ice to use as His weapon in the day of war and battle against the wicked. We hear and read in the newspapers today of how great, hill-like, little mountains of snow are pushing down from the north not only in the northern states of Minnesota, North and South Dakotas and Montana; but now the snow is in the New England States and they are declared to be disaster areas. The announcer of the disaster of snow in the New England States said that there have never been such great quantities of snow. All up and down the coast to the Carolinas, the rain takes up where the snow leaves off.

All around the Southern Border of America, storms are raging. There are tornadoes and heavy rains and more storms are on the way - one right after another. And in the North and Far West and in the East, America is surrounded with the judgments of Allah (God). There are earthquakes and the sea is raging. The Pacific Ocean is now angry and is raging and tossing up great waves as never before.

Why should these things hit America? The Revelations teach you why. It is because America is filled with devils and has such unclean persons living in America. That is true under the symbolism of a hateful bird. Every filthy, slimey, wicked person comes here for a haven, where he can do any wickedness he wants to do—the country is open and welcomes that type of person.

As we see — the few little Muslims, whose name, Muslim means those who have submitted to the will of Allah (God) — how the enemy hates us and seeks to do all the evil he possibly can against us, by falsehood.

These are not the days of Noah, Lot and Abraham, nor are these the days of Moses. These are new times. The enemy does not get away in punishing the righteous just because he hates them.

Allah, the God of Righteousness, is with us and He just Laughs at those who try to fight against Him. He has destroyed whole nations with less than the power of rain, hail, snow and earthquakes. The Holy Qur'an has the record of people even being destroyed by gnats. Allah (God) does not have to have something great. He does not have to go to work and get a block of iron or a mountain and throw it on them. He uses that which is with you, against you.

The forces of nature are great weapons as we see them in play upon America. Storms after storms of snow and ice are rolling in from the North and are pushing great drifts that are just covering up everything. What can you do with a God like that?

Job prophesied that Allah (God) has His weapons stored up to use in the day of battle and war with the wicked. He just takes some snow and covers them up.

The Holy Qur'an says that Allah (God) destroyed people with just cold wind. He froze them. Do you think that you can get away with fighting Allah (God)? No wonder the second Psalms says that He will sit in the heavens and laugh at those who are trying to fight against Him. He will have you crazy. It is true.

The heads of the governments of the Christian world are confused, and they do not know that they are confused. Why? Because their greatest desire was to confuse us. Now Allah (God) has taken the confusion out of us and put it into them.

Eat, America. Help yourself to the dessert that you have prepared for us. You eat it. All praises are due to Allah (God) Who came in the Person of Master Fard Muhammad.

We went to Alabama — and to any state that we go to — we pay a high price per acre of land that our fathers' labor has already bought for us. Now he wants to kill us if we act humble and peaceful and want to buy back some of our own labor.

I laugh at some of the things that I hear coming out of Alabama — and not only Alabama, but every other state in the union. They do not know the time in which they are living. Allah (God) is well able to take the country from you and give it to whom He pleases. It is in your Bible, read it for yourself. He took the kingdom from the wicked and gives it to whom He pleases—those who will bring people into righteousness.

America is surrounded with the judgments of Allah — the four great judgments of rain, hail, snow and earthquakes and confusion in the heads of state.

CHAPTER 36

Four Great Judgments of America

To be plagued with too much rain will destroy property and lives. It swells the rivers and creeks. Too much rain floods cities and towns. Large bodies of water at the ocean shore lines will be made to swell with unusually high waves, dumping billions of tons of water over the now seashore line.

Rain destroys property and kills cattle by drowning them in low lands. Rain destroys the hiding places of vicious beasts and reptiles bringing them out fighting in small towns in peoples' homes and farms.

Rain weakens and destroys railroads, truck line beds and bridges. Rain undermines foundations of all types of buildings. Rain makes the atmosphere too heavy with moisture causing sickness.

Wind with rain can bring destruction to towns and cities, bringing various germs, causing sickness to the people. It produces unclean water by the swelling of streams and destroying reservoirs of pure drinking water used for the health of the people. Rain is a destructive army within itself. Hail stones are also a property and life destroyer.

Snow is of the most dreaded plague when it comes in great drifts from five to thirty-five feet. It buries your property and lives. It destroys your highways, your cities, and your concrete and gravel in towns and cities. It puts a great burden of expense upon the cities. It puts a great burden of expense upon the city to repair it. The cave-in of roofs of homes, the cutting off of homes, the cutting off of transportation, isolating areas, brings about starvation. And communication is destroyed with the icing of communication wires.

Snow looks pretty because of its clean look. Almost everything of nature is beautiful, but it can be turned into death and destruction against man.

Snow is prophesied to be one of the weapons that God will use against the wicked (America), Job 38:22, 23. Hail also is mentioned in the same two verses, where God plainly tells us that He has preserved it against the time of trouble, against the day of the battle and war.

The Holy Qur'an also teaches us that God used snow, rain, wind, hail, earthquakes and fire against former wicked people.

Is America any better than the people we read about in the history that God destroyed? No, she is not as good. These people were not as wicked as the American people.

Earthquakes can destroy towns and cities instantly. America is in the grip of divine judgment. America is in the position toward her once slave, so - called Negro, as Pharaoh was with Israel as his slave. She is in this position because of the injustice done to the American so-called Negro slave, brought to America over four hundred years ago, and refuses to let them go free.

They only say that you are free, knowing within that you are not able to leave them without anything. But the injustice continues to increase. Now they plan death.

So this God was predicted by the prophets to come to the defense of this people (so-called Negroes) in the last days after they served the enemy for four hundred years. The Bible declares to Abraham in

Genesis that God would judge the people to whom his people (Abraham's) would be in bondage.

This does not mean Israel. This means the present Black people, the members of their Black nation, who have and are fulfilling their prophecy.

God, in the Person of Master Fard Muhammad, will not be defeated. The more evil, deceiving, tricking and making of false promises to the American so-called Negro only increases America's divine chastisement — doom.

America knows that her trouble lies in her mistreatment of the Black man, the so - called Negro, but she is too wicked to give up tricking the Negro and deceiving him on false promises. She just cannot stop. The opportunity is too open, and she thinks that there is no one to hinder her.

But God has chosen us to be His people, and He delights in fighting the enemy. According to the history of the former people, He delighted Himself by going forth against them when they exceeded the limit. So it is with America.

They must be separated. America will not agree to see the Negro separated from her until she has suffered divine punishment, as Pharaoh suffered. The same thing that other evil nations suffered before them is now coming upon this people.

She seeks to keep her slaves robbed of opportunity and wealth. She envies success coming to American Negro free slaves. She charges them high prices to keep them down. She deceives them through a few of what we call "Uncle Toms" in the political circle, clergy class and all professional classes.

She offers them little favoritism to help her work

against their own people — the Black people. But they, too, will suffer along with the enemy of justice of the poor so-called Negro.

They must be separated. Envy and hatred are growing between the two people, regardless of their preachings of social integration. The truth must come.

What is better than the program you find I have written. You two, (Black and white) cannot get along in peace since you never have gotten along in peace.

Do you know why the white American does not like to talk with you about separation, and why he calls separation of the two people the wrong solution for peace between the people? He knows that it is promised and that God will do it. Then, why do they not agree with separating themselves from you and me, and we from them? Why are the Black man and white man all over the earth now in disagreement with each other to live in peace? Do you know why?

Oh, foolish American so-called Negro, seek some of this earth that you can call your own to live on in peace. Unite and ask the government for a portion of America.

This is what we need — somewhere to live to ourselves and let the white man live to himself. The two people are not brothers. They are alien to each other. God did not make them brothers to each other.

I ask you, my brother and sister, to learn this and learn it quickly and fly for your life to the refuge of Allah. Come follow me.

CHAPTER 37

America's Land Being Divinely Curtailed

Holy Qur'an, Ch. 13:41, "See they not that We are visiting the land, curtailing it of its sides? And Allah pronounces a doom — there is no repeller of His decree. And He is swift in calling to account."

Black Man in America, there is no one as blind as you are in seeing what is going on against America. I have warned you for nearly forty (40) years that Allah (God) in the Person of Master Fard Muhammad, to Whom praises are due forever, came to me and gave me the knowledge of the truth; and I have been preaching it to you continually.

Now you see what is going on. As America has done, so now it is being done unto her. America has surrounded the countries of other peoples. She has blown their cities to pieces and she has killed their inhabitants. Those who were left alive she put to flight, running for shelter from the destruction by America's might.

It is very sad and horrible to look at the things that America had done, which are now coming on this country. For many years — centuries of years, America has lived a luxurious, wicked life, while hating her Black slaves and depriving them of justice — shooting them down on the streets, on the highways and in the woods and fields, for nothing. She did it just because she felt that she had the advantage; and she wanted to kill Black people, as she was made to do.

Bible Ps. 10:8, "He sitteth in the lurking places of the villages: in the secret places doth he murder the innocent: his eyes are set against the poor."

Up until this very minute, she is seeking to destroy the Black man in America and to deprive him of the freedom to do for self. America never desires a departure of the Black slave from his white slave-master. America wishes only to hold the Black slave in order to continue to treat him with evil.

Pharaoh's hatred and injustice to Israel, in Egypt, in the time of Moses, should serve America as a warning; but she has fallen head long into the throes of the destruction of Allah (God).

America runs to and fro seeking a way out, but she does not try to justify her Black slave for justice and equality among the nations of the earth. America made us into nothing and she used us to mock us before the nations of the earth.

But a God with unlimited wisdom, knowledge and power, is now befriending the Black slave and He has chosen the Black slave to be His people. But the foolish Black people have yet to come into that knowledge; that Allah (God) is their best friend and that He is here to save them from the destruction of a people who have shown enmity and hatred to us all of our lives. America divided us one against the other. The Black man in America is so divided against each other that you seek all of the time to do evil against each other.

You cannot even befriend them lest they take advantage of it. They call you a fool for trying to befriend them, as it was with us, by Midway Technical School.

Midway Technical School came to us for help. We gave them that help to keep them from falling. It cost us thirty thousand dollars to set them free of their back rent and other bills that they had. Take a look at how they have turned on us for the purpose of wrecking all of the beautiful businesses set up for them and others to enjoy on the south side of Chicago, Illinois.

CHAPTER 38

The Fall of America Foretold, Separation is the Answer

Holy Qur'an 81: 6,7,12
And when the cities are set a fire.
And when men are united.
And when the hell is kindled.

The Folding Up is the title, taken from the first verse of that chapter, in which the above verses are found.

When the sun is folded up (Holy Qur'an 81:1) symbolically prophesies the folding up of a recorded work — a record of what people have done, as its use will no longer be necessary. This chapter refers to what takes place in the resurrection.

One party is recorded as a beginning, while the other party is discontinued. We see this clearly being made manifest today. War causes the destruction of civilizations. Wars destroy the cities and towns of a nation. This chapter, 81, of the Holy Qur'an is now being fulfilled.

The sun and the stars, mountains, camels and wild animals are all mentioned metaphorically in the first four verses of this chapter, and are not without significance.

The coming of God referred to by the prophets is to unite a people who have been divided against self by their enemies. He chose these people for building a better world.

The Bible's Revelation refers to the destruction of the beast and his chief instructor, the dragon. The name beast given here is not referring to four-footed animals but to a people whose rule is like that of a savage beast.

Theologians, most of them from the time of Martin Luther (who I think was the author of these terms — "beast" and "dragon") especially the late Pastor Russell and Judge Rutherford (founders of the Jehovah Witness sect) take the term "dragon" to refer to the pope of Rome — the father of the Christian church and the Christian religion.

This is the first time since we have been lost in this part of the earth that we want to unite the Black nations of the earth into one under the guidance of God Who is now present.

Why should the master continue to deceive his slave? He teaches the slave that he is a free citizen with equality.

Why do you (slavemasters) want to hold them; for hostages, prey? You do not need them. Your machines do the labor that the slaves used to do. Why not let them go?

You want to go to war against Allah and the freedom that Allah came to do for your slaves? Before you, Pharaoh had the same idea. He did not want Israel to go free in a land to themselves. Pharaoh lost the war against Allah and was drowned in the Red Sea. The losers of this war will land in a lake of fire, not water.

If white America wanted to free her slaves, she could easily do so. This would be simpler and easier than what she is doing: killing and provoking them through police force, national guards and finally the U.S. Army, as we see in Detroit, Michigan.

America's actions show us two things: Firstly, she

wishes to cause fear among the so-called Negroes, with a display of many deadly weapons, but Allah is removing the fear.

Secondly, she fears to approach her unarmed slave unless she is armed. This has been the historical relation between the white man and his slave.

The white man seeks the leadership of the so-called Negroes to help him keep the dissatisfied slaves subject to him without complaints about injustice. The white man's motto: "Nigger, you should be happy. You are better off than many of your Black kind with a job."

The white slavemaster brought our fathers here to do the slave work. Our free labor has made the white slavemasters richer than their brethren (Europeans). Do they offer us any of this land they took from the Indians?

The twenty two million so-called Negroes should be seeking some of this earth on which to live and build an independent nation out of self. The white master only offers us a job.

Allah, God, has come in the Person of Master Fard Muhammad, to Whom praises are due forever, to free us. The Negro slave must be freed! This is the meaning of the resurrection.

Allah, God, has said to, Elijah Muhammad, that He intends to free the American so-called Negro "at any price."

For four hundred years you (slavemaster) have been killing the so-called Negro without receiving any resistance and regardless of his peaceful way with you.

We, the Muslims, have tried to live in peace here in

America. There is not a single incident in our thirty-six years of history where we have ever made an aggressive move against you, but you have attacked us several times. We have proved to the world that you are impossible to live with in peace.

"Ye have condemned and killed the just and he doth not resist you." James 5:6

You have destroyed many towns, cities and people. As thou have divided the so-called Negro, one against the other, so Allah shall divide you and your brethren.

"As you have done to others so shall it be done to Thee." Bible

"When the cities are set on fire." This is a sign of the end of you as a power.

CHAPTER 39

The House Doomed to Fall

We cannot deny the fact that the Christian West is responsible for this universal corruption in the land and sea.

From the same corruption that their own hands have wrought will come their doom.

The Christians preach that which they do not do and cannot do; such as "Love thy neighbor." I have as yet to meet one who loved his neighbor as he did himself; "Thou shall not kill." I have as yet to meet such a Christian.

They even fight against each other, rob and kill each other, but yet represent themselves as world peacemakers — with whom?

The great deceivers of the world will reap what they have sown. Have they not corrupted many people and nations under the guise of good, peaceful, loving Christians?

The Christian West is full of the worst crimes, practicing evils and indecencies to the fullest and seeking to practice them on other nations as well.

Universal tempters are ever parading before the world their bold half-nude girls and women. They are before your eyes in almost everything. Murder, gambling, robbery, drunkenness, drugs adultery, lying—there is hardly any end to it.

Their land and seas are filled with deadly weapons of war; their islands of the sea are filled with corruption by all the nations of earth, for they are proud and boastful and are now hated and despised according to their wishes.

Their religion Christianity is a curse to us (the Black man) and is full of slavery teaching. They have poisoned the Bible with their adding to and taking from the truth. Now their doom is in sight. It is their own work.

They command the sea with their powerful navies, parking them off the shores of other nations. They secure air bases on their soils to place their deadly bomb - carrying planes within easy striking distances of those whom they fear to be their enemies. Is this not the easy way to make enemies?

Is this the act of a real Christian, the followers of Jesus whom they preach came for the peace of mankind and to teach the sheathing of the sword and the turning of the other cheek?

Where is a good Christian among this race?

They love meddling in other people's affairs. They are in every fight or war— it matters not with whom or where — but yet crying "Peace! Peace!" with every deadly weapon of war to provoke other nations to war.

Shall not the God of Peace and Justice deal with you and your troublemaking as He did with those before you?

I warn every one of you, my people — fly to Allah with me for refuge. As I warned you, the judgment of this world has arrived! Get out of their slave - making Christianity and into the right religion, Islam. The house you are in shall surely fall and never rise again.

CHAPTER 40

The Destruction And Fall

The destruction and fall of the world that we have known is now without a doubt, in process. When we refer to the world, we are referring to the world of the white man, for the world of the Black man has yet to come in.

The world of the Black man, by divine guidance, is now merging in on the old world of the white race. This makes the destruction and fall of the world of the white man imminent.

Here in America we can see nothing but the fall of America. It is no secret. It is obvious to the eyes that are open. If we want to close our eyes and minds and claim that we do not see and understand, then we will be falling ourselves.

This refusal to see is fool-hardy for regardless to how we may desire to see the old world stand, we do not have the power to stave off the destruction that causes the world of the white man to fall.

The destruction and power that is bringing about the fall of the world of the white man is coming from Allah (God). In the past history of the world of the white man, there never was a time of destruction of his world like the present time.

It is useless for you to try to prevent the fall of the white man's world. There is no checking it. The white race has not tried to do the right thing... justice. The doing of justice would have checked her fall (Bible, Jeremiah). But America was never willing; and even at this hour she is not willing to do justice by those whom she has mistreated. She has dealt injustice to her Black once-slave for the nearly five hundred years that she has been in the Western Hemisphere.

America has constantly burdened the poor Black slave with every evil that she could imagine. Her evil scientists who have invented more and more evil practices have not been able to invent anymore evil than that which they have already put out.

Day and night without a let-up the white man mistreats the poor Black slave. Now since heaven and the God of Peace, Justice, Freedom and Equality has come to the Black slave, the white man is trying to make everyone that recognizes the truth deviate from it.

The white man says, "Do not accept it." He makes the Black man a hypocrite against his own salvation. The white man trails the ones who have not as yet accepted the truth of their salvation, and he promises them that which he will never be able to fulfill.

America is falling. She is now losing the power and authority that she was enjoying in foreign lands. Her fall is very visible. Wherever her authority has been exercised the people are now crying out in one voice, "Leave us, leave us; Americans go home to America." The citizens of other countries are telling the American citizens, "Leave us." America no longer has friends.

America and England deposited their little brother, Israel, on foreign soil, Palestine, which is Arab land. They deprived the Arabs of their own land and sent them into exile. This injustice against the Arabs is now costing America the power and authority that she once exercised in the East. She is on her way out of the Near East. This means bloodshed and plenty of it.

In the Near East, there stand navies which are neither American nor British...they are there to drive America out. The skies over there are beginning to thicken with foreign planes, carrying deadly weapons, guns and bombs. They will not be satisfied as long as Israel is in Palestine. The boil has come to a bursting point. We are in a troubled world. We are in a world that is now erupting.

Black man,who was once a slave in America, you have a way of escape. The way out is not on your own terms. It is on the condition that you submit to Allah (God) and come, follow me. This is the only way out. I am the door and I have the key to your salvation. Reject it and die.

We are in a world that is falling. It will soon be going up in flames. In Berlin, Germany, the cold war between the East and West will soon erupt into a hot war. It will never be settled in peace. East and West Germany must and will fight it out with all the deadly weapons that the war-scientists have planned and perfected for the final showdown.

You do not have to worry too much about whether or not America is coming out of Asia. Certainly America is coming out of Asia. The odds are against her staying there. But I warn you, my Black people, my Black brother here in America, that while she is on the way home, we the Black people are standing in the cross-fire. The only hope that we have is to fly to our refuge in Allah (God).

Look at what is going on to the south of us. Look at the many hi-jackings, sticking up of planes. America is afraid to put a stop to the hi-jacking for she knows that she is going to run into more than she expects.

Who would have thought that the big power (America) would suffer such disgrace in this day and time? This is to teach you and me, Black brother, that the great power (America) is become weak and she is falling. I say, Black brother, join onto your own kind. Come follow me, for the world that you and I have known, will soon be known no more.

CHAPTER 41

The Day of America's Downfall

Allah manifests the fall of America. He desires to make America fall as a warning to her brothers in Europe. White Americans and Germans — Allah has taught me — are the most wicked of the white race. The wicked deeds that have been performed and are still being performed by white Americans upon the so-called Negroes (their slaves) are the worst in the annals of history.

They have been clever enough, in their wickedness, to make the so-called Negro slaves love them—though they are their open enemies and murderers. Allah, in the Person of Master Fard Muhammad, to Whom be praise forever, now judges the American whites and is causing Amercia's fall and total destruction. Egypt, under Pharaoh, is an example — fulfilling the signs and other prophecies of the doom of this people as foretold by the prophets from Noah to Jesus.

Moses and Jesus are the most outstanding prophets in the history of the Caucasian race for the past four thousand years. There are several other contemporaries, but Moses and Jesus are the major prophets of the white race's history. The whole of the civilized world today — as prophesied in Isaiah—is against the white man of America. Allah hates the wicked American whites and threatens to remove them from the face of the earth.

Since white Americans, and the white race in general, have deceived the entire world of Black people and their brethren (brown, red and yellow), Allah now is causing these people to wake up and see

the white race as it really is—the created enemy of
the darker people. As we see today, there is a general
awakening of the darker people into the knowledge of
self and the knowledge of their age-old six thousand
years(enemies all over the earth. The American
white race cannot sincerely give the so-called
Negroes (their slaves) a square deal. She only desires
to deceive them.

False Equality

Today America is trying — against her will — to
give the so-called Negro civil rights (which is against
the very nature and will of the white race) for the first
time since the Black man has been here. America
falsely offers him social equality in certain parts of
the country. This social equality consists mostly of
permitting the American Black race to mix openly
with the white man and his woman (the devils). The
actual idea, however, is to grant the so-called Negro
social equality among the lower class of whites. This
is done so that the scriptures — wherein they
prophesy that the white man tempts and corrupts the
so-called Negroes with his women — might be
fulfilled.

God has taught me that the white race was grafted
unalike, and being unalike, it is able to attract the
Black man and Black woman, getting them to do all
the evil and indecency known to the white race.

Doom Prophesied

One of the prophets of the Bible prophesied in regard
to America, ''As the morning spreads abroad upon the

175

mountains, a great and strong people set in battle array." (Joel 2:2). This is the setting of the nations for a showdown to determine who will live on earth. The survivor is to build a nation of peace to rule the people of the earth forever under the guidance of Almighty God, Allah. With the nations setting forth for a final war at this time, God pleads for His people (the inheritors of the earth; the so - called Negroes).

The so-called Negro is the prey of the white man of America, being held firmly in the white man's power, along with two million Indians, who must be redeemed at this time — and will be, if the so-called Negro turns to his Redeemer. The problem of the American Black man is his unwillingness to be separated from his four hundred year old enemies. The problem, therefore, is harder to solve — especially with the enemy trying to fascinate the Negro with his lower-class girls and women, arraying them partly nude before the Negroes in every public news media (cheap daily newspapers, and magazines, radio, TV) and the Negro is quick to imitate.

The problem between these two people — separating and dignifying the so-called Negroes so they may be accepted and respected as equals or superiors to other nations — must be solved. This is God's promise to the so-called Negro (the Lost and Found members of the original Black Nation of the earth). This promise was made through the mouths of His prophets (Bible and Qur'an): that He would separate us from our enemies, dignify and make us the masters, after this wicked race has been judged and destroyed for its own evils.

But, as I said, the solving of this problem — which

means the redemption of the Negro — is hard to do since he loves his enemies. (See Bible: Deut., 18:15, 18; Psalms, Isaiah, Matthew, 25:32; and Revelations, Chapter 14.)

The manifestation of Allah and judgment between the so-called Negro and the enemy of God and the Nation of Islam will make the so-called Negro see and know his enemy and himself, his people, his God and his religion.

Rejection of Self

We hear the statements of Black educational, political, and Christian classes, which express their love for the white man, publicly asking to be his brothers, if not his brothers-in-law. Now this class wants to make it clear to the world that they really love the white race and not the Black race. This means they want to be white instead of Black. The devils have made them hate Black. They reject the thought of Black ever being the ruler or equal with the ruler. They ask boldly for inferiority — not only for themselves, but for their people.

They want to absorb themselves and their kind (especially the so-called American Negro) into the race of white people, thus ending the Black race. It is just the opposite with Allah (God), myself, and my followers. We "want out completely." We want no claim to kinship with a people who, by nature, are not our kin. Read from Genesis to the Revelations in the Bible, and from Sura 2 to Sura 114 of the Holy Qur'an.

By no means are the so-called Negroes and the whites kin. God did not create them brothers, nor did He create them to ever become brothers. One is

177

created an enemy against the other; and since the righteous are more powerful than the wicked, Allah, the God of righteousness, set a time of reckoning for the enemy (the white man) of the righteous.

Separation

We want separation. We want a home on this earth we can call our own. We want to go for self and leave the enemy who has been sentenced to death by Allah (Rev. 20:10-14) from the day he was created. (See this subject in the Bible and Qur'an). No one — white, Black, brown, yellow or red — can prove to me by any scriptures of Allah (God), sent by one of the prophets of Allah (God), that we should not be separated from the white race: that we should believe and follow the religion dictated, shaped and formed by the white race's theologians.

The coming of Allah and the judgment of the wicked world is made clear by the prophetic sayings of the prophets. The so-called "reverends" and the proud intellectual class are doomed to destruction with the enemy if they remain with him instead of joining onto Allah Who loves them and Who will deliver them and the Nation of Islam.

The so-called Negro masses must be warned of the grave mistake they make in following the leadership of those who love and befriend their murderers. This will not get them freedom or civil rights.

America is falling. Her doom has come and none, said the prophets, shall help her in the day of her downfall. In the Bible, God pleads with you to fly out of her (America) and seek refuge in Him (Rev. 18:4). It certainly will change your minds about following a doomed people — a people who hate you and your kind, and who call one who teaches the truth about them a hater. They are the producers of haters of us. We are with God and the righteous.

CHAPTER 42

The Days of Trouble

The days of trouble have now come to us from Almighty God Allah — the God Who is the real owner of the heaven and earth.

Allah (God) created for Himself a heaven and then He let it out to a foreigner (white race) for them to enjoy themselves in it for a while.

They have proved unworthy of such glorious creation, and now the God Who is the owner of this heaven and earth is ready to take over and rule it for Himself.

Never no more, will the earth nor the heavens of the earth be let out, to non-owners.

It is a great wisdom, taught to us, in letting new creatures (white race) try their knowledge of mastering that which they were not made to master — which we knew, when we made them, that they would not be able to master the original creation for long.

For as long as we, the Black people, are of the planet, there is no new creature that could be put in order for ruling that which we already have, and we are in it.

It is such a wise piece of work that has been done. The wisdom, knowledge and understanding of the originator of this creation is just.

There is no comparison anywhere to make — there is no such thing that the originator can put the planet aside out of the whole and let someone else take over.

This race, the white race, has not been successful in ruling according to their will, and according to a real owner, for the white race had to use the originator's material that He Himself had created.

There is nothing of which the white man can call himself the creator.

So, therefore, since the white man continued to make trouble, which by nature he was made to do, we do not see any way out of trying to live with the white man in peace.

The nature of the white man is ever causing unrest among themselves and among us too. The white man just cannot make peace for himself, because of his nature.

Today, God has decided that we, the Black people, cannot get along with the white man in peace, and that the white man must be removed.

The white race wanted to remove us, the Black people. But in order for the white man to remove us (the Black man) he would have to remove the whole entire heavens and make the heavens void of anything like life.

Then from a void we would have to start all over again and create life, for the life in the universe is life that we, the Black people, have established.

Therefore, to get away from our own life, (which was created by the Black man) so that a new life could come in, we would have to rid the space of life, which belongs to us, the Black man — and when the space was rid of the life that we (Black people) had created, another one would have to create life of his own making.

We, the poor Black people here in America, must be changed into a new and different people altogether, so Allah God Who came in the Person of Master Fard

Muhammad, to Whom praises are due forever, taught me.

But, not a complete make of us — we will be renewed from what we are in now — and we call it a new thing. There will come a day when we (the Black people) will have a completely new thing for man and earth and the heavens above us! But, according to the scientists, God will cause this to grow into a new thing — not a complete destruction of the old where there is no root to grow something from — not at this time'

The things that Allah (God) would like to do now, and will do, is to destroy the works of the devil — as the devil would like to destroy God's work, which God has created.

The devil cannot destroy God's creation because the devil had no part in the creation of the first creation. Since the devil had no part in the first creation, this makes the devil unable to lay hold to the power that would destroy the first work (of God).

The main thing, which I keep mentioning enough to make you disgusted is — something for the Black man in America, who has spent his life long in sleeping, in ignorance of the knowledge of that which he is in.

But as soon as the Black man can awaken to the knowledge of this that he is in, then he can lay hold to that which he did not have knowledge of, which is that the Black man is the creator of the first creation.

Allah (God) wants to put the Black man back into power and the way the Black man can be put back into power is: Allah has to make the Black man all over again to master the power after giving the Black man the authority.

Look at the poor once-pitiful Black man in America — look at how he strives to reach for himself, and is now making a fast progress in that which God leads for Him to Understand —

The Black man's conversation is changed — the Black man's way of thinking is changed — his actual physical form is changed — It is a great thing that has come to the Black man in America. The Black man in America is getting happier and happier.

It is not hard for the Black man in America to get rich, for he is getting rich from his own wisdom. No one has given him anything.

As the Bible teaches you of the Prodigal Son — 'no one gave unto him, but he is getting rich, so fast, that God chooses the Prodigal Son to become the head of the house that he strayed away from!

The future of the Black man is so beautiful that we can hardly comprehend it! The biggest thing that stands before us is qualification — and readiness. Let us get qualified to master the house that God is giving to us, before someone tries to rob us of that mastering of the house. If they rob us of the mastery of the house, I am sorry for us.

I say to you, Black Brother and Black Sister, do not be foolish. The kingdom of heaven will be given to you and to me. Have patience to receive it.

But, to get the house into our service, it is like a mother giving birth to a baby — the baby must mature in that which he is in. As a baby matures in the womb of the mother in order to be born, so the Black Man must mature to be born into a new world that the Black man must build himself. These are the days of trouble.

183

CHAPTER 43

Plagued by God, America is Doomed

With the end of the rule of the white race over the Black people of earth in sight — face to face — we have to deal with each other according to the actual facts which exist between the two nations (Black and white).

With the nature and desire of the white race to continue their rule and subjection of the darker people even though the white man recognizes these facts, he will continue to try holding onto his rule; his subjection; his thinking of what he has acquired under such rule — that which is his and he cannot give up the prey — his concession — the merchandise which he has exploited out from under the noses and eyes of the real owners (Black man).

He is willing to shed the blood of his own people and that of others to hold onto that which he calls his legal possessions. The spirit aroused in the Black man says, ''NO'' — that the continent and what is on and under its surface belongs to him and his people (Black nation). This spirit and knowledge is now not only confined to Africa and Asia, the Black, brown and yellow people, but it actually is now arising in the American so-called Negro, the true lost and found brother of the Black man throughout the earth — whether it be Africa or Asia, he is the brother of them all.

It is the desire of the white race to continue to hold power and authority over Black Africa, whether it is in Rhodesia or elsewhere. They will just have to give it up. England, Germany, Italy and France — especially England, France and skeleton Germany —

seem to be the die -hards.

The white men in Rhodesia would be acting wisely if they would realize that one day, sooner or later, they must pack up and leave. Wherefore I quote the Bible prophecy concerning the separation of nations, again today, as it was before: "Every man must go to his own." This is the clearest and most direct justice that God and man could agree upon.

The white man cannot live in luxury unless he has the Black man and his place of possession in subjection to his will. But, as I repeatedly say in this paper and in all of my writings, "You cannot make God and His prophets liars," nor can we reverse the time of their prediction in which these things would take place. So the time has come.

This is nothing but justice; that we have possession of what is our own. The white man is conscious of the fact that he deceived the Black man of the knowledge of the Black man and his possessions. But that particular authority was given divinely; temporarily. But, by the same Divinity, it is now being taken from the white race.

The white race is facing doom because she will not act according to justice and righteousness — which was not by nature put in her. But this is known and her race is frightened concerning her future, as we see here in America.

The white man recognizes his coming doom and many of them would rather die here than to go elsewhere, outside of America, to try to defend what they call "their own independent sovereignty." Some have poured gasoline over themselves and committed suicide by setting themselves afire.

This is a very new and open act of a people who want every other people (Black, brown, yellow, and red) on earth to fight their wars to save their independence.

A ruthless and brutal people like America, England, and Germany should be ashamed in this modern time to look for these people, whom they have robbed, killed, murdered and brought under subjugation by force, to think that today they should be so soundly asleep that they ignore the time and the authority that they can unite, as the European has been doing against Black Africa and brown and yellow Asia.

As the Book says to the white race: "As Thou hast done, so shall it be done unto thee."

The white man must return to Europe and concentrate on that continent for his future — or else concentrate on his death instead of his life — for they can no longer rule the Black man. The Black man now knows where his home is and he now is rising up to take possession of that which is his.

CHAPTER 44

America's Doom Feared

Allah in the Person of Master Fard Muhammad, to Whom praises are due forever, for finding and offering to set us in heaven at once, on our submission to Him entirely!

We fear the doom of America that is now cutting her to pieces. The prophecy teaches us that her doom will come in one day—death and mourning came in one day. One day means one year.

Even after that she shall utterly be burned with fire. Divine prophecy is that America will suffer isolation from the nations of the earth.

The Revelations of John of the Bible prophesy of America's doom. America is spoken of under the savage name of a beast and dragon who will oppose the Messenger of God and all those who seek to follow him.

Beast and dragon are the names used to represent America because of the nature and the characteristics of this people—evil and haters of his Black once-slave.

The beast or dragon trails the woman seeking to destroy the Messenger and his followers, the new converts. The Messenger of Allah is referred to as the woman with the new born baby, with a vicious beast-like enemy trailing her (the Messenger of God) everywhere that he goes.

The beast does this to prevent the Messenger and His followers from making progress in making friends with his own Black people who will help the Messenger to convert and unite his Black People—not only in the United States of America, but the whole world of the Black Nation.

To unite and fly out of our enemies who seek to destroy and kill you and me night and day does not just mean leaving America. But it means also to leave the ideology and all that America represents.

'And the nations (Europe and Asia) stood afar away off for fear of her burning (U.S.A.) and for fear of her Divine Plagues.

To you, my Black people, the end is now.

Who said that you were going anyplace? Heaven and hell are both a condition of life. They are not places. The devils make hell for you, and God, in the Person of Master Fard Muhammad, to Whom praises are due forever, makes heaven for you and me.

CHAPTER 45

America Hastens Her Own Doom

The ultimate aim of this world should be known to everyone, especially the righteous. We classify the righteous as being the people who belong to the right God, the God of righteousness, truth, freedom, justice and equality of the nation of righteousness.

Today, the so-called American Negroes must be resurrected and made to know and understand the fate of anyone who will follow or be deceived by the arch-deceivers.

The strongest and most powerful weapon the arch-deceivers have at their disposal is to deceive the world of righteousness (the Nation of Islam). They do not stop at the common, ignorant Muslims, but reach also for the scholars and scientists of Islam, who should be aware of their trickery and deceit.

We are in a world that is passing out of existence—and she is putting up a fight (war) to destroy the nation of righteousness. Be aware! To try to oppose the success of Allah's truth only hastens the doom of falsehood and its teachers.

The world of evil makes its first attack on the world of righteousness, thereby clearly showing herself as being the enemy of righteousness. When she thinks she has built up a strong enough force to attack the righteous, she does so which, as I said before, hastens her own doom. Falsehood cannot be victorious over the truth in the day of truth. The resurrection is a day of truth. The resurrection is a day of truth, as it triumphs over falsehood.

The archdeceivers force war against themselves. Their ultimate aim is to do as their people always have done — try to destroy the preacher of truth and those who believe and follow him. This was the aim of Cain when he slew his brother, Abel, and the aim of the dragon when he sought to destroy the woman (the Messenger), as it is written in Revelations 12:4.

The lost-found members of that nation should be taught to know the ultimate aim of this world. God has visited them, and has prepared a teacher (in myself) to teach them, thereby making it easy for them to understand and recognize this world and its secret, ultimate aim. It is even given in the Bible, in Revelations 12:9. There it speaks of the members belonging to the righteous nation, and shows that through deceit, Satan causes them to become as himself — against the truth, peace, justice, safety and security one would enjoy if he only were not deceived.

Under deceit, the weak minded — who have no understanding or knowledge of the archdeceiver (the devil, satan) — are made preys in the hands of the archdeceiver. This will bring about war as a showdown between the God of righteousness and the God of unrighteousness (the devil). It already has begun.

God must fulfill His promise to show Himself as God over all the powers of heaven and earth, and men on earth. As it is written (Thessalonians 2:9), "He comes after the workings of Satan." Satan has been given the power, knowledge and authority to deceive as many as he could before the appearance of God or the universal manifestation of the presence of God. He was given this power in the beginning, according to Chapter 2 and 7 of the Holy Qur'an, and according to the Bible in Genesis 1:26, Revelations 6:4,8, and

Revelations 12:3,4.

We have known all our lives that the devil was a great deceiver, an enemy of God; and that he wished to be the victor, with his knowledge of superior arts in deceiving the people of God.

He desires to cast them down, disgrace them and make them accept his deceit before the very face of God in the general resurrection of the dead.

The so-called American Negroes—as I have repeatedly taught in my articles, sermons and lectures to my people — are the spiritually dead. They have been touched and paralyzed to death by the arch-deceiver through his missionary teachings, his literature, his personal conversation and by accepting his advice.

God has given to me a very strong and invincible truth that will defend, protect and prevent you from falling victim to the arch-deceiver. Read these, and treasure them; they are your life. Ignore them, and it is your death.

CHAPTER 46

The Great Days,
The Terrible Days of God

We must not forget how we are warned by prophecies for one hundred years and for one thousand years that an end must come to his world.

The rulers of this world must be removed and the crown must be taken off and placed upon another head, and they will rule in justice and righteousness.

The people of this world have now become so wicked and so fearful of the consequences of their own rule until the almost thoughtless vision is gone, and fearfulness has taken hold of the people.

Their head is going to and fro to the nations of the earth to find a way of peace between the heads of the nations. "A Great Time! A Troublesome Time! A Terrible Time!"

The hearts of the people all begin to weaken and to fail because of what is going on and what they see is coming!

America and her people have lived so rich and so joyfully in wickedness, murder, robbery and hatred of one another until it has hardened their hearts so much they are made to think that they can make friends and live on with those upon whom they had no mercy.

They crushed all the weak nations of the earth with their power and brought them into the clutches of slavery. They forced other nations to bow. They pushed their borders around the earth as Nebuchadnezzar did in his days and time.

But, in those days Nebuchadnezzar boasted — and think over it, England made the same boast. England used to boast that the sun did not set on her empire. Take a look at England, today. There is no British Empire for the sun or moon to set on!

This morning, May 30, 1972, the radio news-announcer said that they found mines in the Chicago River. This makes it altogether more frightening; for if a mine should blow a ship up in the city limits it would be dangerous to the lives of the people.

And just think over this. The Chicago River runs through the down - town section of Chicago, Illinois! No one wants to frighten the people more, but the frightening of the people sometimes does good.

"The Great Days, The Terrible Days!" People are just being shot down on the streets; right in their homes; or while walking the streets. They are blown down as though their lives are nothing. "The Great Days, The Terrible Days!"

CHAPTER 47

America's Dreaded Destiny

America and her people have been here, according to history, since a few years after Columbus, the explorer. She conquered the aboriginal red Indians, the original owners of the land, whom she found here and took it for a home for herself and kind. She has continued conquering until her conquering power has gone around the earth affecting every civilized nation; submission to her will. She was successful in forcing other people to bow to her will—whether they liked it or not.

Now it is the hand of God which is after America to force her into submission — a hand from which we have no defense as it is written and prophesied in the Bible, under the name of Babylon.

Jeremiah 51:25: "Behold, I am against thee, O destroying mountain, saith the Lord, which destroyest all the earth: and I will stretch out mine hand upon thee, and roll thee down from the rocks, and will make thee a burnt mountain."

Jer. 51:53 says: "Though Babylon should mount up to heaven, and though she should fortify the height of her strength, yet from me shall spoilers come unto her saith the Lord."

America is under a destruction similar to that of ancient Babylon. In the Bible, Jeremiah, Isaiah, and Revelation of John prophesied concerning her. Babylon, there-mentioned is a future Babylon, and not a Babylon of the past.

America has enslaved all of the so-called Negroes and her evil mistreatment of them is similar to ancient Babylon's enslavement and mistreatment of the Jews, according to the scriptures. It took the hand of God to bring the king of Babylon and his people into submission to the power of God.

He brought the surrounding kings and their power against ancient Babylon in the prime; the height of her glory—the hand writing on the wall—the casting of Daniel and his followers into a fiery furnace; making drunk the people of God with their strong wines and then mocking them—so has America done to the so-called Negro.

America makes him drunk with wine, whiskey and beer and then laughs at him. She put him into the fiery furnace — burned him at the stake while sitting around with her families, drinking intoxicating drinks and laughing at the burning flesh of God's people.

There is no justice whatsoever. As Revelation gives it, "She made all the world drink of the wine of her fornication." But an end is coming to such evil doings.

America has lived in peace — so far as foreign war is concerned. She has destroyed other peoples and their towns and cities. She has leveled them to the ground. She is still prepared to do the same with her great stockpile.

She says she has enough bombs and destructive weapons to destroy all human beings on the face of the earth three times, and still have some left. Of this she boasts. But Allah (God) has said to me that He will destroy America. He will bring her to her knees (humiliation).

The destruction sent to ancient Babylon and recorded in the Bible is the answer to most of what He has said to me will come upon the now rich America. Rain, hail, snow and earthquakes—these weapons all belong to God. America, how do you fight an army like this?

The four mentioned weapons of Allah (God) cannot be ignored. The whole year has been a year thus far of Allah (God) plaguing America day and night with storms, rain, floods; killing and destroying property.

And now the coming winter — hail has been falling in some places the size of golf balls, baseballs and footballs.

The rain continues to fall in places and a dreadful snow blizzard is now in the workings. A cold wind is brewing in the North to come against America, as it is written and prophesied in Job 38:22-23: "Hast thou entered into the treasures of the snow? or has thou seen the treasures of the hail, which I have reserved against the time of trouble, against the day of battle and war?"

Earthquakes are now again to be recognized, touching America lightly — but nevertheless they are here. With all of her wealth and preachings of Christianity, she has not been a good Christian herself. As Jeremiah says: "Arise, get you up unto the wealthy nation, that dwelleth without care, saith the Lord, which have neither gates nor bars, which dwell alone."

This corresponds to America. She lives situated between the two greatest bodies of water of the earth, the Atlantic and the Pacific. And she is very careless. She rejoices in her evil and filth as though she is self-protected from the divine hand of God.

Jer. 50:31 prophesies: "Behold, I am against thee, O

thou most proud, saith the Lord God of hosts: for thy day is come, the time that I will visit thee." Allah (God) is visiting America with great destruction which He has to pour upon wicked America.

After their mistreatment of the so-called Negro for four hundred years, she desires now to deceive them and to cause them to suffer with her and share in her doom.

Jer. 50:6 — "My people hath been lost sheep: their shepherds have caused them to go astray, they (white and Black preachers of Christianity) have turned them away on the mountains: they have gone from mountain to hill, they have forgotten their resting place." (their native people and country).

Jer. 50:7 "All that found them have devoured them: and their adversaries said, We offend not, because they have sinned against the Lord, the habitation of justice, even the Lord, the hope of their fathers."

Since the white man has made the so-called Negro as wicked a person as himself now, these are the words that he speaks: "They are just as evil as we; therefore, Allah God is against them, too." The so - called Negro repeats the same and says the white man is no worse than the so - called Negro.

The white man has opened all of his doors and avenues of temptation to lure the Negro in for total destruction.

Again we have a warning to leave a people with whom God is angry as the people of ancient Babylon were warned to do.

Jer. 51:45— "My people, go ye out of the midst of her, and deliver ye every man his soul from the fierce anger of the Lord."

All of the plagues, destructions and judgment which Allah (God) used to destroy the wicked and disobedient from the time of Adam until this day will be brought upon America. Then she will be burned with fire. This is the time of trouble that shall bring America into insanity.

CHAPTER 48

The Dreadful Times of America

America, and especially North America, has entered into the time that was predicted by Moses and the prophets between him and Jesus. In the 24th chapter of Matthew there is a prophecy made by Jesus of the present time of America, without mentioning her name.

He referred to the country as a world, because this part of the earth is referred to in many places, by prophets and by Jesus himself, as a wilderness. The name America is not yet 500 years old, so the prophets referred to it as a wilderness in their prophecy.

It is terrific. I use the world "terrible" because it is not a thing that can be described as something mild, or something that is moving slowly, nor something that can be recognized so easily by the common people.

It is clear to all who can see that America has reached the stage about which she always has been warned. She always has wanted to keep it a secret, because of her so-called Negro slaves.

She never desired for the slave to know too much of what was in store for her, because of her enslaving and mistreating her slaves. She has reared them for the past 400 years—and she knows them. She knows how they think and how they react to her teachings, and she knows their fear of her. She knows her slaves, but the slaves do not know America—their slavemaster.

The great, dreadful and awful day (doom) is now in the doors and windows of America, and of the church—the religion of America. As long as Christianity worked, America thought she was safe, because it is one of the most deceiving and outright misleading religions of the world.

Allah (God) taught me that, if carefully examined, everything in the religion of Christianity is designed to make a slave out of Black people. If Christianity was in a wet rag and wrung out, every drop would write slavery for the Black man.

The world knows this now but the spiritually blinded, deaf and dumb American so-called Negroes, to whom I am calling and appealing to reason. I am calling them to reason with me on the truth and their own salvation, that is now in truth of self and kind and of the enemy of self.

There will not be an end to the clashes between black and white in America—and throughout the world—until wrong, evil, murdering, deceiving and robbing the poor Black man of the earth, is destroyed and righteousness and justice are practiced.

This is the day of God Almighty to set up justice and equality throughout the earth. He is to free the Black man—the American so-called Negro—from his deceitful, evil and murderous enemies.

America wishes to oppose Allah (God) in this work of bringing justice and freedom to her once slaves, but this is just what Allah (God) wants. He (Allah) wants America to attack Him, to get the fight started and to bring His judgment against her with the fullness of His strength and power.

America is bringing about political gloom. Here politicians are unable to carve out a future for America. The plan of deceiving the so-called Negro politicians to work against their own freedom, justice and equality (salvation) that Allah (God) has brought to them, is making the so-called Negroes in high offices become the enemy of his own people's freedom, justice and equality.

Such offices are held out as a bribe to get Black politicians to work against the spread of the truth of their salvation. They are happy—and their boss knows that they are—to have a place near him in such offices just for the purpose of trying to oppose Allah and His Messenger in freeing the poor Black man who is in the mud.

This is causing the political confusion and complete destruction of the house divided against itself.

I am asking, in the name of Allah, that the American government agree on the separation of her once slaves and their master. Of course, Allah (God) is sufficient.

We want a home on this earth we can call our own. We do not want to be slaves anymore to white people. We do not want to be free "Uncle Toms" for white people. We want to do something for self and go for self. However, America, with her blind, deaf and dumb politicians and clergy class of the so-called Negroes, will bring a swift destruction upon their heads, along with the doom that is inevitable against the enemy.

It is not twenty years in the future—nor fifteen years. Let no one deceive you. It is here at our doors now. The dreadful plagues and confusion of America are beginning to boil. The fuel making it boil will not cease until it is boiled down to the last of the dregs.

The present promise of a better future that America is making to the so-called Negroes will prove to be false. All of her false promises to the American so-called Negroes, will be short-lived by both—because the time of her doom has approached. America would have to do a miraculous thing of justice (a square deal) to turn it back.

A fantastic show of tempting the Negro to filth and evil will not work. It takes justice to work, to postpone the dreadful days of America. America's loss of world friendship is speeding her doom.

CHAPTER 49

Lull Before The Storm

I am afraid for you, that you will receive what the people before you did receive. Allah (God) is very angry with America and the tricknology that she uses on the dead to keep them dead. You are very disappointing to Allah (God) and to the original Black man who knows himself (a very few) of course.

The false show of a glorious future that the wicked is putting on is at hand. We must remember Daniel's prophecy, that "at the end of the war desolations are determined." But before this happens Allah (God) will bless the people with a good time, as He did the people of the past, who wronged themselves and who did not pay attention to the prophet's warning among them. Allah (God) destroyed them. They thought that they were fooling Allah (God) but Allah (God) surprised them!

He made the people rejoice for a short time, with a show of great prosperity and at the height of their great prosperity suddenly, He destroyed them. This is the merciful law that Allah has put in nature.

Allah (God) lets a dying person rally before the end. America is going to do the same. America will rally and people will think that she is going to have a great future, and then the end will come in that kind of time.

America's end will not come while she is going around with her head hanging down and with heart aching and failing because of the things that are coming on her nation. No, she will be made to enjoy good times.

The stock market, going up, and lots of shares being

sold — this makes any man think that everything is all right. But, this is only "The Lull Before The Storm."

And the Bible warns America of what happened before her. Ancient Babylon enjoyed a full ruling position at her time. But King Darius came against her at the time of her full enjoyment of wealth, drunkeness and her laughing at the slaves that she had made of Israel. King Darius came with his army and overcame the sleeping guards who were sleeping on the security of their life.

The Bible prophesies that the enemy will say, "Come, let us go up and destroy her whose city is not fenced in." And they will come from afar. They may come at noon-day, or they may come at rising in the morning, or in the afternoon. But, nevertheless they will come at a time that you thought not.

After the war — "and unto the end of the war, desolations are determined.....and that determined shall be poured upon the desolate." (Bible Dan. 9: 26-27) I want you to know that, that which will be poured means: it is the deprivation of you, America, of your ever getting back into power again to attack the nations of the earth.

Europe will become one of the worse war areas of all the world; more dreadful than Viet Nam and other places that you are planning on going into. Asia will look like child's play when compared to what is going to happen in Europe. The prophets say, "Woe to the land that is shadowed with wings." This means America whose sky is filled with planes.

Most all of the judgments and troubles which are pointed out in the Bible are pointed at America. Study them for yourself.

America, right up to today — with all of her battles with her outside enemies, never loses sight of the inside—her poor old Black Slave—she does not want him to do anything. She wants him to be deceived. She does not want him to accept his salvation that Allah (God) is offering the Black once-slave, here in America.

Allah (God) Is Offering the Black once-slave heaven at once. This He has proven to everyone that believes in Allah (God) and follows me. I am the Door. By no means can you get by except you come by me. Your prayers will not be heard unless my name is mentioned in them. I am saying that you cannot get a prayer through to Allah (God) unless you mention me in your prayer. Try it and see. I am satisfied that those who know this will bear me witness.

I have the key to your salvation, and I have the key to your hell. I can, if you will let me, pull you out of hell and set you into heaven. Then I can keep you in heaven; or I can keep pushing you and push you into the punishment of hell until you acknowledge that there is no God but Allah Who came in the Person of Master Fard Muhammad, to Whom praises are due forever and that Elijah Muhammad is His Servant.

There is no escape for you today. The only way is through me to Allah (God). Me first, for you cannot get to Allah (God) without getting to me first.

"The Lull Before The Storm"—America is trying with all of her might to hinder you from getting into heaven. America makes promises to you, and she makes promises to me, but she does not intend to fulfill them.

Some of America's financial people promise to loan

us millions of dollars; but when it comes time to do so, they vanish. But the day will come when we will be able to do the same thing to them. It is entirely up to them to make good of this day for themselves and their people by submitting to the truth themselves as the Bible says, "The Gentiles shall come to the light of thy rising."

America wants to destroy God and me, and she wants to destroy you by deceiving you against following me. America lifts up all of my hypocrites and advises you to follow them, while she knows that you will be the loser.

Look what she has done for Malcolm. America named universities after him in order for you to follow Malcolm. Malcolm turned from Allah (God) and me and started to follow them. America will lift up anyone of you that will disobey Allah (god) and myself and come to them. You see how they are doing. Everyone that is a hypocrite to Allah (God) and me, America will raise him up for you to follow. America will glorify his name.

Malcolm was no lover of white people. He only lied to them in order to get a chance to fight me. But he was not a lover of them—Malcolm was a double-crosser. He tried to get to me with their help, as it is written and prophesied that he would do. His name is not written there in the name of Malcolm in the history — another name is used but his work is there in the history of the hypocrites in the life of Muhammad. He tried to take advantage while Muhammad was sick. You find this in the writings of Washington Irving and even some science writers of Islam. They can tell you Malcolm's history.

But the enemy fools you. He did not like Malcolm, but with Malcolm working against me, he used Malcolm. They knew that Malcolm had learned the history of me, and he was not able to change it.

And even if the enemy would glorify them, they will come to a naught for their time as a ruling-power over Black people, is up. They knew that better than Malcolm did. They set up for worship all hypocrites against me. Suppose we would worship China and Russia against them? But we do not worship them for Allah (God) is most sufficient—more sufficient than all their nations.

Allah (God) does not see them as a power and force against him. They are so little and weak in their power. They cannot fight against Allah (God) and win. The more you fight against Allah (God) the more you will lose yourself.

From the Bible, and from this chapter, from now on, if you do not know that he is tricking you by making you to follow hypocrites—it is your doom.

Just watch it. He trails me. He goes down to the Bahamas and everywhere that he thinks that I am going, or where I have been. This is written. I do not fault him for doing what is written of him. I try to do that which is written of me. I do not fault him for what he is made by nature to do. Nor should he fault me for what by nature I am. But I fault you if you let this little transitor of this life and our enemy deprive you of a great future for yourself.

We could buy hospitals and places to educate and train our people into the superior education of the nations of earth. But you would rather give your money over to white Americans and let them spend it on what they want to, and they pay you a little interest. We offer interest too; the highest of interest. But you do not trust us.

So we will build right along without your help. We are going to be the winners. It is prophesied that we who believe will be the winners. And my work, that was prophesied of me before I was born, you see it today.

Try and find a successful one who is working in opposition to me. None of you who are trying to aid the devil against me will be successful in doing so. And the devil knows that. He is not trying to do these things himself...only with you. He knows that he will not be successful in stopping my progress..not him nor several times his number, as long as I am with Allah (God) and He is with me and that will be all the days of my life.

CHAPTER 50

Fire Fed With Fuel

The subject of this chapter is taken from the Holy Qur'an Chapter 85:5.

We do not hope for peace as long as we add to the war that which serves as fuel to a fire. The fire cannot go out as long as we keep it burning by adding more fuel. A dying, burning fire is increased when more fuel is thrown into it.

There are a lot of people who are so anxious for peace so that they can return to committing that which they lack and love — idling, sport and play.

The world that we live in desires first of all to hide the truth to keep the Black man who is made blind, deaf and dumb by the scientific tricknology of the white race, so that the white race can continue to carry on the same deceiving and wickedness that they have been practicing.

How can we expect peace where the method used to bring about peace is the same method that started the war — instead of finding a right solution and then practicing the right solution?

I say these things for the sake of my own Black people, for they are so ignorant to the knowledge of the truth of the time in which we are living. What they would like to do cannot be done, for the time to even continue to do what you are doing, is up.

We must remember again the prediction of the Bible. It has foretold these times, if we understand the Bible. It most certainly teaches us that there is no peace for the wicked.

There is no people who preach such a thing as peace and as being true followers of the prophet Jesus, as much as the white Christians do. Day and night the air-waves are full of their preaching. To hear them, you would think that they are the prophets Moses and Aaron. As the words of the Jesus put it, "They sat in Moses' Seat."

The white Christians are great deceivers. The pope of Rome cannot bring peace to the Christian church, for he is not enjoying peace himself.

So who is that people then that the Bible prophesies of in the Book of Isaiah that "He will extend peace to them like rivers?" Surely it cannot be the present Christian white race for they are the ones who are breaking the peace.

"Fire Fed with Fuel" — leaving your own home and country you go to another man's home and country to make trouble for that people and then accuse that people of being the trouble-maker. It is the attacker who is guilty of that which follows the attack.

I say to you Black people, you can get away from that old misunderstanding of the time. You are not living in a time in which you may be expecting a settlement of the war that will give you what you have always been used to — sport and play and foolishness.

Actually now is the time that you and I should be wise enough to understand that we should think for self and do for self. If you do not know how to do for self, you should follow the man to whom Allah (God) has given that knowledge to teach you how to do for self.

With the oceans filled with the fleets of the white Christians and the skies clouded with their death-dealing planes over other peoples' territory could you tell them that they should submit to you for peace? If you are able to force them to their knees or to destroy them, then I say yes. If that was the situation then I would say that they should submit and let you triumph.

But you cannot force them to their knees. They have been preparing for a war like this for nearly a century; or rather I should say, they have been preparing and working faithfully for a half a century to entertain the attacker with the same type weapon and better weapons than the weapons you are attacking them with. If you resort to worse weapons they have worse weapons also.

So we are in a time when argument to the contrary of peace is like heaping fuel on a fire — it keeps it burning. We are living in an evil time.

I believe, and maybe many hundreds of thousands believe as I do, that the President of the United States of America had good intentions toward the citizens of America when he took over the presidency, but the time is against him.

For the past four thousand years and more Allah (God) has already given the prophecy through the mouth of His prophets of the doom of the wicked. Now is the time and we cannot do anything but take it, and it is dangerous to add fuel to an unwanted fire.

THE FIRE IS THE WAR!

CHAPTER 51

Men's Hearts Failing: Fear

How true the prophecy of Jesus, Lu. 21:25-26 concerning the present time. We bear witness that the sea and waves are roaring and that fear is now coverning the nations as shown by the unusual heart failure that is now occurring among men. These are signs of the end of the present world.

The sea and ocean are heaving up tidal waves to un-imaginable heights that man has never witnessed before on earth. This is another plague that is upon the wicked.

Since the Holy Qur'an teaches that the judgment would be such that the earth itself would act as though a revelation had been revealed to it because of its perfect obedience to the Law of Allah on that Day.

Allah will use the power that is in the earth and in the sea against the world of evil. The white race think that they have control of the power of the earth, sea and air.

It was prophesied that for a time they would subdue and have the use of the power of the sea and ocean until He Comes Whose right it is to rule.

The heavens and the earth belong to Allah (God). Now it is His time to rule.

There is much prophecy concerning the terribleness of the judgment of the wicked.

The power that is in the water is in the Hand of Allah (God) to use it against whom He pleases. The earth, wind, rain, snow and ice and earthquakes are controlled by Allah (God).

It is a fearful sight to see the Display of His Power with the forces of nature bowing and submitting to His Will. I should warn you that this is now coming into action against the Western world. There will be the destruction of whole fleets at sea. Those which are capable of lying on the ocean and sea bottom will be destroyed.

The die is set, with a foolish people, who like, in the time of Noah, could not see the sign of the rain, bringing on the Flood even after the clouds began to darken the sky. They did not see the on-coming rain until it actually started to rain.

So it is with America. They pay no attention to the signs of the judgment that is now taking place. As the Bible prophesied in Rev. 16:9, They..."blasphemed the name of God, which hath power over these plagues...". How many in America and the city of Chicago disbelieve and even mock and swear at the Name of Allah, Who has power over the forces of nature on land, sea, and air.

Allah (God) is now doing as it is prophesied: Holy Qur'an, Chap. 13:41, "...visiting the land, curtailing it of its sides." The foolish still are foolish until he is cast into a narrow place and cannot turn to the right or left, as it was with the donkey that Baalam was riding. He came to a narrow place between two walls. He could not turn around. He had to stop face to face with the angel or be destroyed. Bible Nu. 22:23-26.

Let it be remembered that Allah (God) came forth for the Redemption (to Deliver) the American Black People from their tormentors. Whether we like it or not, He Will Do this. This is the Work of Allah (God) which is in effect.

Let America use the history of the fall and destruction of ancient Egypt and her Pharaohs. Let their histories serve as a warning. They all were brought to naught for their evil done to a people whom Allah (God) has chosen for an example of these last days... the lost-found Black slaves and their slave masters.

The Holy Qur'an, Chap. 30:41, is perfectly true in its prediction of a present day nation's sea and land power. "Corruption has appeared in the land and the sea on account of that which men's hands have wrought."

The most grave mistake that the Black Man is making today is his trying to hold on to the belief in the return of Jesus, or that he lived and preached the saving of the white man's world. This is false. Jesus did not preach this. See Bible, Jn. 17:9. Jesus had a few disciples. Jesus also cursed the Jews, not to mention that he was trying to save them...or the Caucasian people.

They are teaching a tricknology that the white man uses to deceive the Black Man. They do this so that our people will not understand that Jesus declared himself against the world of the Caucasian race, Bible Jn. 8:44. He also declared that the word of truth had no place in this white race of people. They have proved this to be the truth by their mistreatment of you and me.

The white race has never worshipped any prophet, before or after Jesus as a Divine Man of Allah (God). It is against their very nature to do this. That is why they kill all of the prophets they are able to kill. They deceive the people against believeing in the prophets of Allah (God), for they were made in their nature to be the enemy of God and His Representatives.

Before the time is out, they will be forced into

submission to the will of Allah (God). This will not be done for the purpose of converting the white race Allah (God) will force them into submission to prove that He is able to make everything bow to Him in submission.

This is in fulfillment to the prophecy, Bible Is. 45:23, "...unto me every knee shall bow; every tongue shall swear.." The Bible says, Mt. 25:32, "And before Him shall be gathered all nations:..." The Holy Qur'an has a similar prophecy, "that you shall see all nations kneeling before Him.'

This includes everybody, regardless to their color. Everything in the universe obeys the natural law in which it was made subject to by Allah (God).

On the coming of Allah (God) He now makes everything bow to Him, whether you believe or disbelieve. Holy Qur'an 3:82. It does not make a difference to Him whether you are the devil or the righteous..all must bow in submission to the will of Allah (God), on the judgment day. We are now living in the days of judgment.

Black Preachers, you will waste your time in leading yourself and those who follow you to hell by holding on to Christianity. Rev. l9:20. You cannot keep them in Christianity.

Christianity was not the religion of Jesus, Moses or any of the prophets who came before them.

It would have been a farce on the part of Allah (God) to have waited until just 2,000 years ago to give the right religion to the world of man.

Allah (God) gave man the right religion, Islam,in the beginning of His creation of the heavens and the Earth. Allah (God) has not changed. His religion is Islam, entire Submission to His Will.

CHAPTER 52

Hell Erupts

Why are the nations angry ? Who are the nations that are angry at the resurrection of the dead?

The 18th verse of the 11th chapter of Revelation in the Bible plainly teaches us that these nations are angry and mad because of the rise of the dead and that God Himself was the source of the power behind the Resurrection or Rise of the mentally dead people (the Black man).

It is these slave-holders who have been the real cause of the mental death of the people the Revelation relates to as being deprived of justice. God comes to give them justice and to justify them as being equal to their slavemasters as human beings. As you know from the four hundred years of legal slavery and free slavery of the American so-called Negroes, they have never been recognized even as human beings. As one devil says, they are only three-fifths of a human being.

It is true that the history of our treatment by the devil slavemaster practically made our parents and ourselves less than human beings. This is why I teach that the main rights we should seek first are human rights.

The American so-called Negro fell in love with his slavemaster and his slavemaster's children because of unalike attracting them and their brothers in Africa; therefore, the manifestation of the enemy devil in the Resurrection makes the dead to see that which causes them to be mentally dead.

In the parable of the donkey who balked upon

meeting with the angel, he saw that the burden he had been carrying on his back was false (Baal). So in the resurrection of the mentally dead so-called Negro, they are rising to the knowledge of self. This knowledge makes them balk or refuse to continue carrying the slavemaster as something to worship. This has angered the slavemaster as the donkey's refusal angered Baal.

Baal set about whipping and beating the donkey to force him as usual to carry and respect him as his master. This use of force to compel the once-slave (the Black Americans) to remain with them even now in order to make them members of their society is only false recognition of the Black American, this lost and now-found people of the Black nations of Asia and Africa.

This continuous cruelty by their white slavemasters, inflicted upon the American-so-called Negro, has angered God as the cruelty the Egyptians inflicted upon the Israelites during the time of Pharaoh angered Jehovah. This is a repetition of Israel's history and of Pharaoh's evils in these modern times: the appearance of Jehovah and of Moses, the servant of Jehovah, to announce to Pharaoh the end of Israel's slavery. Pharaoh became angry and went to work and tried to obstruct and bring to naught Jehovah's delivery of Israel through his servant Moses. This brought Pharaoh to his end, and he and his army were cast into the Red Sea because they tried to prevent the freeing of Israel by their God Jehovah.

The angry nations refer to white America and Europeans, who are also enslavers of the Black man.

Take for instance the part that England, Belgium, Germany, France and Italy have all played in the enslavement of Black Africans and Black people throughout Africa, Asia and here in the Americas (North and South America).

There is no such thing in the nature of white people as justice and freedom for Black people; especially not for Blacks in the Western Hemisphere. Now their anger is running them mad and they are attacking and killing each other. There is no such thing as peace among them, nor can they produce peace for others. The Holy Qur'an refers to this condition as the kindling up of hell (Chapter 81:12)

Never before have you witnessed the evil that is spreading far and wide every hour of the day in America and Europe; England and America being—not the first—but the chief—slavemakers of Black people. They dislike the idea of having Allah dispose of their power over the Negro, though they knew this was coming (the loss of their slaves).

This is the time of the increase of knowledge. God has given the Black man of America more light into this increase of divine knowledge than any Blacks elsewhere because He chose to make for Himself a great nation out of the former slaves of America.

White America is angry at God for resurrecting the Black slaves into the knowledge of self and his slavemaster. This means that they are entering into a war with Almighty God Allah to try to oppose the truth of God preached by the Messenger of God. Read the second Psalms.

CHAPTER 53

The Great Commotion

The great commotion of the government and people of America; the civil unrest, insurrection, mental excitement, and noisy confusion — there is no action that is being taken, nor can there be any action taken, that would bring the people to a better condition of civil action.

The white American people have practiced evil and injustice to the man in the mud, the Black slave, for so long that they think that there would never be any divine action taken against them, for such evil and injustice. But this is what is now affecting—it is the actions of divine justice for the poor man (Black slaves).

Allah (God) in the Person of Master Fard Muhammad, to Whom praises are due forever, has the power, and He is using His power on the wicked to bring them to their knees. Allah (God) is the greatest and there is no equal to Him. Allah (God) can take us by our own way of thinking and spin us as though we are a play-toy. We cannot fight a successful fight against Him. He is too powerful. He listens in on our thinking and He is capable of making us to think and to do that which He desires to be done.

The great commotion today is witnessed by the nations of the earth, for it is America whom Allah (God) is after for her mistreatment of the poor so-called Negro (lost-found original Black members of their nation). America mistreated and killed her Black once-slaves for sport, but America's day is drawing to a close and she will not have the freedom to mistreat the Black once-slave, much longer. As the mistreatment of the Egyptians practiced against Israel came to an end, so will the mistreatment of the Black slave by white America come to an end.

America has so blinded and made deaf and dumb, the Black Man in America, her Black once-slave, that she makes empty promises to the Black slave and he will accept her false promises and forsake the true promises of Allah (God) in the Person of Master Fard Muhammad, to Whom praises are due forever, Who is here offering us heaven at once.

The great commotion will continue in America until this commotion has destroyed the power of opposition.

CHAPTER 54

The Calamity

The title of this chapter is taken from the Holy Qur'an, Ch. 101:1-4.

"1. The calamity!

2. What is the calamity?

3. And what will make thee know how terrible is the calamity?"

In the English language, according to Webster's Dictionary, the word calamity means, "a state of deep distress or misery caused by major misfortune or loss, or a great event marked by great loss and lasting distress and affliction."

Such calamity is now prevailing in America. It is getting worse daily.

The third verse of this Chapter (Holy Qur'an 101:3) asks a question: "And what will make thee know how terrible is the calamity?" The answer is given in verse four:

4. "The day wherein men will be as scattered moths,"

We do not have to ask anyone whether or not this warning of the Holy Qur'an is now being fulfilled. We see the fulfillment of this prophecy with our eyes and hear with our ears, these great calamities that are now striking America. We see the great division, the great disagreement, disunity and murder of men. We see the great amount of raping and murdering of girls and women. There is great robbery and thieving going on every hour of the day and night.

There are great storms and adverse weather

conditions. There are minor earth tremors and hailstorms. There are signs and wonders of signs being displayed in the heavens, in the earth and on sea and land. There is unusual behavior of children. There is unusual love or dislike of children by mother and fathers and the destruction of the process of childbirth. There is the great calamity of starvation and great destruction of health and of lives by the use and adminstering of poison drugs, which is practiced upon those who are free and those who are bound.

What has been known as America is threatened today with total destruction. America is destroying herself in her effort to destroy her Black slave. The water and air of America are being polluted by chemico-bacteriologists.

America's scientists of war conduct dreadful experiments on how best to kill human beings by the millions and wipe out the life of whole continents.

These are the days of fulfillment of prophecy of not one, but of many calamities. But in all of these preparations of the destruction of human life by the devil,...Allah (God) too has plans to save His people.

Allah (God) has claim over the Black slave as being His people and the white slave-holder is angry because of the loss of the Black slave by virtue of this claim.

Allah (God) comes to take the Black slave away from the enemy white slave-holder and join the Black slave onto his own kind again. The enemy white slave-holder hates this, but Allah (God) has the power to force the enemy white slave-holder to submit to His will.

It is the will of Allah (God) that the enemy white

slave-holder let the Black slave go free. Allah (God) promises concerning the white slave-holder and the Black slave, Bible Is. 43:6, "I will say to the north, Give up; and to the south, Keep not back: bring my sons from far, and my daughters from the ends of the earth;" (America)

Since Allah (God) has now claimed the Black slave (given them the truth), Allah (God) has called the Black slave (who has accepted the truth) by His name. The Black slave who has accepted the truth of His greatness in being one of the righteous aborginal nation of his kind belongs to Allah (God). The Book must be fulfilled wherein it prophesies that He will claim them to be His own; elect.

At such time as the destruction of America, if Allah (God) has not chosen some of the people of America (the Black slave) to be His people, there would not have been any flesh saved from America.

The Bible, Mk. 13:20, teaches us, "And except that the Lord had shortened those days, no flesh should be saved; but for the elect's sake, whom he hath chosen, he hath shortened the days."

It is vital ...the Black slave must know that this is the time of the judgment of both the white slave-holder and the Black slave. The Black slave must learn to know his place in the judgment. The place of the Black slave is with Allah (God) and his own Black people. The Black slave had been deprived of knowledge of his God and his own Black people.

Allah (God) has come and brought the Black slave the truth. If the Black slave refuses to accept the truth, he will be destroyed for willingly and knowingly rejecting the truth when the truth has come in his midst.

Calamity! calamity in the country of America. No secret can remain hidden, for the chastisement of Allah (God) will not let you hide it.

As one writer prophesied in the Bible (Is. 18:1), "Woe to the land shadowing with wings..." This prophesy is referring to America which has a cloud of planes shadowing the skies over America almost daily.

CHAPTER 55

Can America Exist?

The coming of the white man to the Western Hemisphere was for the purpose of expansion away from his brethren in Europe. Europe was divinely given to the white race as a home when they were driven out of Arabia six thousand years ago to abide there on that continent until their day of reckoning comes to them.

These are the days of reckoning for the white race as their religious scholars and scientists agree. But because of their nature (evil) they cannot help doing evil things against the righteous. They make war against the righteous (the Black man) to prevent him from accepting righteousness and the doings of righteousness.

Today the Black man in America is a prey into the strong, powerful hands of his enemies (the children of their slavemasters).

For four hundred years the slavemasters have mistreated their slaves and now in the day of their redemption they are doing everything possible to deceive them from accepting their salvation that Allah now offers to the Black man of America.

So strong is Allah's love for us that He now desires nothing but a total destruction of America.

They hate me with a bloody hatred, and they try to kill me for teaching the truth to my people. They do not want the Black man of America to enjoy freedom, justice, and equality.

Look what they did to Martin Luther King, a man who was trying to be their brother, a man who publicly taught that he did not want to draw the white man's blood. He said if there was any blood to be spilled, let it be the Black man's blood. His word came true. Poor Man.

He was without the knowledge of self, his God and religion and so filled with fear of his four hundred year old enemies, that he could never get salvation for his people from their enemies.

America has been blessed ever since her fathers came across the Atlantic out of the confines of Europe until this day. Now for her evil done to her slaves, God threatens her with total destruction.

America and Germany are the most evil of the white race. These two governments have been blessed, but they have not shown any worthwhile respect to Allah for His blessings.

Allah caused people out of all nations of the earth to come to America (They came seeking a heaven in her but those who came were evil too), as the Revelation in symbolic language teaches (Revelation 18:2) "And he cried mightily with a strong voice, saying Babylon (America) the great is fallen, is fallen, and is become the habitation of devils, and the hole of every foul spirit, and a cage of every unclean and hateful bird." There is no people nor country on the earth who will fill this prophecy better than America and her people.

She has become a house filled with evil practices with every member of the nations taking part.

Yet she has been blessed with her great harvest of food which is enough to feed the nations of the earth; with her great advancement into the heights of mechanical knowledge and with her great wealth in silver and gold that enabled her once upon a time to command the value of silver and gold of the world.

But, as it is written, in all of this growing up of wealth and power, the ax of justice was laid at the root of this great tree of prosperity and authority of the nations of the earth to be used by the Holy One to put a stop to their evil practices and injustices to the righteous.

America has prospered from the labor of her Black slaves. She pays the Black man high wages and salaries and then takes them back from him through the high cost of living. This high cost of living or trying to live according to the way the white man lives, keeps the Black man down. And when he has acquired the education of the white man but is unable to compete with the white man, he becomes dissatisfied to the degree of creating trouble to find a way to self prosperity against the will of the white man which is to keep the Black man in a condition of poverty, want and disregard as an equal human being. Yet, while the white man teaches that all human beings are created accordingly, at the same time he robs the Black man of a chance to be the equal of other human beings?

Can America exist with all of her wicked doings against the Black man in America in a state of inequality with other human beings?

The continued existence of America in the way of government and power over people other than her own depends on the way she will continue to treat her once slaves (the Black people of America) due to the prophecy of the Bible from Moses to Jesus and Muhammad.

The Prophetic sayings of these prophets teach us that a coming showdown between Allah (God) and the slave holders of His people (Blacks of America) must come to pass.

The time has arrived of this prophecy of a Defender, coming to defend the prey (so-called Negro) who is held in bondage by the white slave holders who have and are still mistreating the prey to the extent that the world is in sympathy with the prey for justice.

Now it is prophesied that a just Ruler will come—and He has come—to set up a rule or kingdom under the law of justice for a people who have lived under the law of injustice by unjust rulers. This must be fulfilled if the next government for the people universally is going to be under such a glorious rule of Freedom, Justice, and Equality.

It is natural that the old ruler will oppose a new ruler coming to remove him and his authority to rule the people. He will fight to keep his place and authority over the people. This is why Allah threatens His opponents with the final declaration of war that will end the opponents' opposition to His law of righteousness.

I have been writing for many years of the coming doom of the world of Christianity and mainly America who is the root and the cause of this present judgment of America.

The judgment of America is due to the way that she has treated the so-called Negroes (Black people of America) for four hundred years. The very hour in which I am writing, America is still mistreating her once slaves with the worst kind of treatment ever accorded human beings.

America practices the way of her fathers' treatment of the American so-called Negroes, under what she calls a law of freedom but this "freedom" is only in word—not in practice.

The slavemasters children's blood, heart, and way of thinking toward the once slave is the same as their fathers'.

They find it so free to beat and kill the once slaves (so-called Negroes) at will that they will continue this practice of mistreating and murdering the slaves day and night because there is no law of justice for the Black man of America who was the property of the fathers of America's white citizens.

America never thinks in terms of being equally punished for the wrong done to a so-called Negro.

The Bible's parable of Baal riding the donkey must be remembered. When the angel went to settle the unjust mistreatment of the donkey by Baal, the angel found Baal still beating and forcing the donkey to carry him, right in the presence of the visiting angel, who was carrying a sword to bring about justice between the two.

It is almost impossible to say that America can exist. If America is to exist (America's ruling power) it would make prophets of the Bible and even the Holy Qur'an prophesy other than the truth. It is impossible to make them out liars who wrote the doom of the race, that it would come at a certain time and that certain time is now known.

The time can be prolonged if the Great Mahdi, the Messiah, that the world had been looking for to come for two thousand years, desires; for He does what He pleases.

This does not mean that He would change the idea of the doom and destruction of America. But if He pleased He could extend her time if she did almost a miraculous thing like submitting to the righteousness taught and delivered to the mentally dead slave (the so-called Negro). This is the only way America could exist; by bowing in submission to the will of God, taught by His Messenger.

The time that we are now in is a time of the anger of God against the evil-doers. It is a time that the God of righteous rejoices to repay the evil-doers for their doings, and to reward the righteous for their righteousness. Therefore, to curb this set day of doom, demands for the doing (righteousness) which, by nature, was not put in the white race. But they may yet be smart enough to bow to put a stay to their execution for a few days longer; not by intermixing with her slave to enjoy as long as they are blind, deaf, and dumb, and do not understand. This act only hastens their doom, while the foolish blind, deaf and dumb so-called Negro does not even know that he is being blind, deaf and dumb to his slaughter.

There is no such thing that their evil will rule peace. Also the wicked, according to the prophets Jeremiah and Isaiah, are the ones who have destroyed the peace from among men.

My advice to the white man is to make haste. Get in a hurry, if you want to live. Bow and submit to that great truth and righteousness, the will of Allah.

CHAPTER 56

What Will Be The End of The War?

Many of you may think that if America ends her war in Asia this will bring peace and prosperity to the people of America. Perhaps, someday, there may be a lull in the war, but not now.

If America and Asia can find a way to bring about a cessation of the war between each other this does not mean that peace and prosperity is assured; not at this time.

There is still the cold war in Berlin, between America and Russia and in other parts of Europe, to be reckoned with. Europe will become a dreaded spot when America leaves Asia. It is true, as the prophets have predicted, that America must come out of Asia, or be thrown out.

Each, America and Russia, the two most powerful war-factors of the world, is seeking to maintain their rule over the nations of earth, and even to conquer outer - space. This will not last long. In their travel and investigation into space, Allah, (God), is permitting them to peep into His great, unequalled creation of power and might, the heavens and earth. The Holy Qur'an, teaches that when Allah (God) gets ready to destroy a people He opens the doors of heaven to them. He gives them a peep into His great wisdom and secrets. But this does not mean that this adds power to the enemy to be able to war against the Creator. The reason for all of this is due to the fact that Allah (God) is setting up a kingdom of righteousness, freedom, justice and equality.

Black Brother, do not look for a high paying job

drawing a big roll of money, after the war, unless with the help of Allah (God), you prepare this for yourself, which I advise you to do.

The most dreadful divine judgments that have ever been witnessed by man are now coming on America. America is the divine target because she could have bettered herself in the divine eyes of Allah (God), Who came in the Person of Master Fard Muhammad, to Whom praises are due forever. But America did not and will not better herself, as it is written and prophesied, concerning Ancient Babylon and Egypt. "We would have healed Babylon, but she is not healed:..." Bible, Je. 51:9, (because she was not willing to do justice by her captive Jews from Jerusalem).

So it was with Pharaoh when Allah (Jehovah) went after Egypt, (Bible Ex.). Pharaoh refused to give justice to Israel and made war against Allah, (Jehovah), and His Prophet, Moses, to prevent, Israel, from going free of Pharaoh's enslavement of them.

CHAPTER 57

The War: America Cannot Win the Victory

It is impossible for America to be the victor in this universal war because of divine intervention against her. Although she has enough deadly material manufactured to try to win, can she win against Allah (God)?

She boasts of her material and being able to destroy the people of earth thirty times. If she was left free to use her material maybe America could win, but the divine die was set against her long before she ever became America.

She can try and boast of her idea of mind to deceive her Black slaves, but she will deceive herself and them. America is made manifest, by Almighty God, in the Person of Master Fard Muhammad, to Whom praises are due forever, that she is total and deadly enemy against her once slaves.

For many years, I have written that America's greatest sin is her evil done to her Black slaves. Allah (God) intends to repay her for what she has done.

She deceives the Black slaves right at the point of total destruction. She tries to woo the so-called Negro with false and temporary promises by offering him high political jobs to keep him from turning his attention to self and kind. The Black politician could and should use his political knowledge to benefit self and kind.

White America isolates the Messenger of God from their minds with these false promises and makes them to hate the Messenger of God and to work against him although the Messenger of God is working for the interests of the Black slaves.

The eyes and ears of Allah (God) are open, looking and listening to their actions. It is not necessary for Allah (God) to use mechanical devices. Allah (God) is physically real and He has real physical eyes and ears. He is capable of seeing and hearing everything we do and say. He has power to defeat us in our plans which are against His plans.

The American slave-holders want to deceive the so-called Negro into believing that Allah (God) is not paying attention to them. The white man wants them to believe that he is the god that they should pay attention to.

I warn my people who believe in the idea that the white man is the god they should pay attention to. You will come up the loser.

Allah (God) is backing me up in the work He has given me to do. The work He has given me to do is for your own Black salvation. If you think that you have salvation with the white man, then go ahead with him. I am not here to force you against your own will, but I want you to know that if you are looking to white America for your salvation you are headed with them to your and their destruction.

There is no hope for America to win the war. There is no hope for the Black man in the future of America for America has no future for herself. She will not be able to win the war.

The scholars and the scientists know that America cannot win. It is not just I, alone, saying this.

Scholars and scientists will tell us America cannot win and we know by divine prophecy that America cannot win.

If it were just Russia, China, Viet Nam and Korea

using their judgment of how best to destroy each other, maybe America could win; for she has as much as they have in war material and scientific preparation.

America is capable of going out of the atmosphere of the earth and to fight them from there, but she will not be able to go out of the atmosphere of the earth and destroy the Black Man of the Earth.

It is only a mistake that one should believe in America's ability to build a way-station in the air or on the moon for she will not be able to use it against us, for the divine plan is set to destroy her.

We have many things out there in space that can be brought into action against America or any other nation today; for Allah is the Greatest.

CHAPTER 58

The Mother Plane

The Mother Plane was made to destroy this world of evil and to show the wisdom and mighty power of the God Who came to destroy an old world and set up a new world.

The nature of the new world is righteousness. The nature of the new world cannot be righteousness, as long as unrighteousness is in its midst.

The same type of plane was used by the Original God to put mountains on His planets.

Allah (God) Who came in the Person of Master Fard Muhammad, to Whom praises are due forever, is wiser than any god before Him as the Bible and the Holy Qur'an teach us. He taught me that this plane will be used to raise mountains on this planet (earth). The mountains that He will put on this earth will not be very high. He will raise these mountains to a height of one (1) mile over the United States of America.

This reminds us of the prophet's prediction of this time of the destruction of the old world and the bringing in of a new world: "Behold, the Lord, maketh the earth empty, and maketh it waste, and turneth it upside down, and scattereth abroad the inhabitants thereof." (Bible Is. 24:1)

There are planes in various nations today, but this is the mother of them all.

Why? Because this type of plane was used before the making of this world.

Why should God make such a sign of His power to destroy a nation? Because this is the final destruction of that people who have opposed God in His purpose and aims for Justice and Righteousness.

The white race is not a people who were made righteous and then turned to unrighteousness; they were made unrighteous by the god who made them (Mr. Yakub).

Allah (God) Who came in the Person of Master Fard Muhammad, to Whom praises are due forever, taught me that this Plane is capable of reaching a height of forty miles above the earth. His words could have been a sign meaning forty years, in which the Plane would go into action, and not referring actually to forty miles. Allah (God) does not speak one word that does not have meaning. Every word that He speaks has meaning.

The Mother Plane, according to what has been described of it by the devil scientists, is capable of not only staying up for long periods of time; but it is also capable of eluding the scientists. They want to attack and destroy it; but if a plane did get close enough to attempt to carry out this purpose, it would be destroyed instead. The white man has learned that this is not a plane to be played with. Planes come out of the Mother Plane.

In the 1930's Canadian newspapers reported that they saw the wheel (Mother Plane). It came down out of the sky. They admitted that it looked like a great city, and that something came down from it; it appeared to be a tube, but the tube-like thing went back up again.

Allah (God) Who came in the Person of Master Fard Muhammad, to Whom praises are due forever, taught me that after six months to a year, the Mother Plane comes into the gravity of the earth. It takes on oxygen and hydrogen in order to permit it to stay out of the earth's gravity until it needs refueling again.

EZEKIEL'S PROPHECY
OF THE WHEEL

Ezekiel saw the Mother Plane in a vision. According to the Bible, he looked up and saw this Plane (Ez. 1:16) and he called it a wheel because it was made like a wheel. A Plane that is wheel - shaped can turn in any direction, at any time. He admitted that the Plane was so high that it looked dreadful, and he cried out, "O wheel" (Ez. 10:13).

Ezekiel saw great work going on in the wheel and four living creatures "And their work was as it were a wheel in the middle of a wheel." (Ez. 1:16). And when the living creatures went, the wheels went with them: and when the living creatures were lifted up from the earth, the wheels, were lifted up Ez. 1:19. The power of the lifting up of the four creatures was in the wheel.

The four creatures represents the four colors of the original people of the earth.

There are five great powers of the nations of the earth. These five Powers are the Black, Brown, Yellow, Red and white. Of the four Original Powers, the Red is not an equal Power. The vision shows the four creatures being lifted up from the earth. When the wheel was lifted up, they were lifted up and when the wheel stood, they stood. This means that they waited upon the movement of the wheel.

In Ezekiel's vision concerning the wheel, he said that he heard the voice of one tell the other to take coals of fire and to scatter it over the cities; this means bombs. It could mean fire too, however. The Plane is to drop bombs which would automatically be timed to burrow quickly to a position of one mile below the surface of the earth where they are timed to explode.

Allah (God) taught me that these bombs are not to be dropped into water. They are to be dropped only on the cities. It will be the work of the wheel. The wheel is the power of the four creatures, namely the four colors of the Black Man (black, brown, yellow and red). The red Indian is to benefit also from the judgment of the world.

We must remember that God comes to separate from the righteous that which is hindering the righteous from making progress and to destroy the effect of the poison of that which has opposed the righteous. The effect of the poison will be fully destroyed after the destruction of the source of the poison, which has poisoned the righteous.

It is like one being bitten by a rattlesnake. Quickly medication is administered in order to minimize the effect of the poison upon flesh and blood until a complete cure is effected; and the patient recuperates and is well again.

It is useless to try to ignore Ezekiel's vision of the wheel, for the make and the destructive work of the wheel was foretold before it came to pass.

The disbeliever believes that which he sees present and not that which is prophesied to come. That is why he is the loser and takes the course to hell, because he disbelieves in that which is prophesied to come about a particular day.

This is what the enemy is trying to do today with the Black Man. He is fascinating him with sport and play and indecency and the doing of evil to keep him from going to the God Who is present.

You never thought the day would come when you would see your wife, mother and old grey-haired women walking down the street today, half-nude. A few years ago they would not have dared to come out into the public like that. But now they do so because the devil has put his approval on this kind of attire. They desire to please the devil. They do whatever the devil bids them to do. The devil desires to take the Black man with him to his doom.

Let us not classify the prophets as liars and ignore their prophecies for we may cause our self - destruction through belief in the devil instead of belief in the God of Righteousness.

There is no known equal of the Mother Plane. This is the reason why she is called the Mother Plane.

The Mother Plane is made for the purpose of destroying the present world. She has no equal.

Do not marvel at the make of this plane, since it is from the God Who made the universe of floating planets and stars which are supported only by the Power of Allah in their rotation in their orbits.

Allah (God) Who came in the Person of Master Fard Muhammad, to Whom praises are due forever, taught me that the Mother plane is a little human-made planet. Is it not simple for Allah (God) to make a new planet if He wants to?

The Mother Plane is capable of staying out of the earth's gravity for a whole year. She is capable of producing her own sphere of oxygen and hydrogen, as any other planet is able to do.

The Mother Plane carries the same type of bomb on

her that our Black scientists dropped on the planet earth to bring up mountains out of the earth after the planet earth was created.

The knowledge of how to do this has not been given to the world (white race), nor will they ever get this kind of knowledge. The knowledge of the world is limited. If the devil would get this type of knowledge we could just say that we are goners. However, they are not able to attain this type of knowledge.

What does a six day old baby (white race) look like trying to compete with a six year old child (Black Nation)? For the six year old child can run all out in the yard and play. He can eat solid food. The power of the six day old baby is limited.

The knowledge and power of this world's life (white race) is limited. The world of the white man was made from what he found and what he has seen and learned from the work of the original Black man. The white race is far from being able to equal the power and wisdom of the original Black man.

The Mother Plane and her work is a display of the power of the mightiest God, Master Fard Muhammad, to Whom praises are due forever. Master Fard Muhammad, to Whom praises are due forever, is the Wisest and Best Knower; He is the Mightiest of Them All.

"O wheel," says the prophet Ezekiel. She was so high up in the sky that she looked dreadful.

She is capable of staying away from you who plan the destruction of her. She is capable of confusing you who would try to reach her with your means of destruction.

There are scientists on the Mother Plane who know

what you are thinking about before the thought materializes (Holy Qur'an Ch. 50:16). Therefore, it is impossible to try to attack the Mother Plane. She can attack you, but you cannot attack her.

The Mother Plane can hide behind other stars and make herself invisible to the eye because she does not have to wait on a power from the earth. She can produce her own power to go wherever she desires to go in space.

The Mother Plane is not like your little bullets or cameras which are powered by your limited power.

The Bible prophesies that today Allah (God) wishes to make known to us that He is God. He wishes to be respected as the superior God. He wishes all life in the universe to know that He is the greatest.

The Muslim recognizes Allah (God) to be the greatest. He always repeats "Thou art the greatest. There is no god Like unto Thee, None deserves to be served or worshipped besides Thee."

O mighty wheel. I repeat, that there is plenty of significance to the make of the Mother Plane. There is much significance to the course of operation of her work.

Space here in this book is limited, but what Allah (God) taught me concerning the Mother Plane could be put into book-form.

O wheel, made to rock the earth and to heave up mountains upon the earth. O wheel, destroyer of nations. No wonder the prophet Isaiah prophesied that the "earth shall reel to and fro like a drunkard..." (Bible; Is. 24:20.)

Let us seek refuge in Allah (God) from the destructive work to come from this Mother of planes.

CHAPTER 59

The Decision

Holy Qur'an, Chapter 78:2 "Of the tremendous announcement."

"The Day of Decision." We are now living in the time in which we must decide on what we shall do. It is very important that we arrive at a solution, come to a definite agreement.

You, Black man of America, are holding back your decision. You are waiting because of the people who have brought this Day of Decision to us by their way of rule. Their rule is in the way of injustice.

Now the God of Justice is before us, and we must decide upon whether or not we will accept a change of rulers or remain under the present rule that is passing from the scene.

We must decide rightly in order to relieve the people of the pressure of injustice. Let our decision be for the benefit of our present and our future generations.

We have no objection to that person who makes up his mind to remain in what he is already in. However, this announcement of great importance is laid before you and me so that we may come to some kind of decision: agreement on what we shall do about the truth of this announcement.

The announcement is the truth. It is asking us to decide on whether or not we are going to accept the truth or remain in falsehood. It is called "The Day of Decision." Decide this day which God you shall serve—The God of freedom, justice and equality or the same old wicked god whose rule Allah (God) is here to bring an end to.

The wicked rulers veil the eyes of the people with falsehood so that the people may take falsehood for truth and truth for falsehood. This is what the Bible and Holy Qur'an teaches us.

All of the important announcements made by the prophets from Moses to the present day — the enemy of truth has deceived the people and made the people think that they were listening to falsehood. They made the people think that the prophet and his God were too weak to prevail over falsehood with truth.

What is said here in this writing is directed to the Black man in America. He is the real one who must decide on whether or not to remain in what he is in or accept a better world that is ruled by the God of freedom, justice and equality.

My Black brother, I want you to know that you are in a pitiful condition here in this day in which the announcement is being made to you to make up your mind about what you are going to do. In plain words, I wish to write here and tell you that you do not have a long time in which to decide on what you want to do.

Thinking that you have a long time to decide is the mistake that people made in the past. Noah's people and Lot's people were the losers for ignoring the announcement from these worthy prophets. They waited, for they thought that what they had was going to continue to be.

We here in America do not have to wait and see; for America is folding up under divine chastisement and destruction is taking place before your and my eyes. Also, the Bible and the Holy Qur'an prophesied of these days and what is going on. These days are the days of judgment of Allah (God) against the wicked.

To see 'more' may mean the end of your life and my life as it was with the people of Noah and Lot who waited to see 'more'. They could not come to a decisive point of agreement. They waited and maybe you too will wait.

To wait for the truth to be fulfilled means that we will suffer the consequences of the truth — for not accepting the truth. "The Day Of Decision."

As there were opponents of the prophets in the past, we have opponents of the prophet in this modern time. With all of the warning that was given before these days, we could make our decision so easily.

Remember the people of Noah had no prophets nor scripture before Noah. Again, remember that even as late as the time of Moses, the people of Moses, the Israelites, had no previous scriptures before Moses.

You, Black brother, are better off. You have all of the scriptures that were given to prophets throughout the whole six thousand years of the white man on the planet earth. And then you will be so foolish as to delay in making a good decision until you see something happen and as the Holy Qur'an and Bible teaches us, or until you see the angels coming in the clouds of heaven before you make up your mind. But still probably you would reject that. Surely it will come in the clouds of heaven. But as the Holy Qur'an teaches you, it will not be a good day for you who have waited for such time. When the angels come in the clouds of heaven they will not be coming to do anything like preaching or giving you further knowledge. It is prophesied that on the Day of judgment the angels will come to execute judgment on you for not believing and to save those who do believe.

The preacher, the Messenger, is the first to be judged. Then the angels come to execute judgment on those who did not believe the Message. The angels in the time of Lot are a good warning to you today. Those people were lost, for the angels came to execute judgment on the opponents and disbelievers of Lot and the cities of the plain where he was living.

"The Day Of Decision" only means the resurrection and judgment of the present world. As Jesus prophesied, as it was in the day of Noah, Abraham, and Lot, so it will be today. They were eating and drinking and having a "good time" as they called it; but it is not a "good time"; it is a wicked time.

The history teaches us that by waiting they were the losers; but yet, it will be the same, today. It is the same, for it is going on now. You are rejecting this truth and you are accepting falsehood instead.

Naturally the enemy of truth is angry with the Bearer of the Truth because by nature the enemy was not made of truth. He was made of falsehood.

But again the Book (Bible) teaches that "Whosoever believeth, the same shall be saved." This is truth, whether he is white or Black. If a white man, woman, boy or girl believes, even though by nature they are not the real righteous, their faith will get them out of the hell that Allah (God) threatens this world with. And their time will be prolonged. I am sure that you know this. They also know this. A remnant of them will escape if they have the faith in Allah (God) and His Religion, Islam, as Jesus prophesied in the Bible,...that even though an enemy give one of his least ones (believers) a drink of water, and that being an act of goodness, The God will Not deprive that act of goodness of its reward.

Make up your mind. Come to a right decision. I warn you.

CHAPTER 60

When Ye Shall See All These Things

Jesus prophesied that when we see the fulfillment of the prophecy of this time, then we should know, by such acts of the people, — strange actions that we have never witnessed before — carried on by the people — "Know that it (the end) is near, even at the doors."

The Bible prophesies in Daniel and Matthew, saying that this is a time that man has never seen before, and man will never see such time again, after this time!

Strange happenings — the prophecies of Jesus said that parents will be against children, and children will be against parents. Do you not see these things being fulfilled today, right in our eyes?

Not only are parents against children and children against parents, but parents are murdering their children and children are murdering their parents!

In some families, the parents kill the children and then commit suicide themselves! This is going on, today, in the old U.S.A., where the gospel of Jesus is preached every hour of the day somewhere in the land!

In this time, in which we are now living, there is no respect for dignity — the President leaving the country to travel afar, to meet with rulers of foreign countries to discuss the strange things that are happening, and the strange things that will happen, between the nations.

The beautiful and rich country of America, to which many people of Europe and Asia migrated, seeking refuge — in this country, as the prophecy is now coming into fulfillment..("...in that day and time, everyone will begin to go away from America, instead of coming to America!"

As the Revelation (Bible) teaches us of the prophecy that "they will stand afar off and see the fire of her (America's) burning and for fear of it they will lift up their hands and their voices. They will lament for her!"

America's trade is cut off and all of her delicious and delicate things that she used to have in trade — it is all gone! In one hour (one day) it came to pass, here in the Western Hemisphere!

The most wicked people who ever lived on the earth are in the Western Hemisphere, as the Bible teaches us that God said, that to Him this is like Sodom and Gomorrah.

He (Allah) (God) did say that "The wickedness of the day of Noah and his people, and Lot and his people, (the Sodomites) was no more than child's play compared to the wickedness of today, for they are highly educated—they are scientists at making wickedness for themselves."

Day and night, up and down the streets, people are killing, murdering each other! We do not know very much about what is going on in Europe, but we do see it right here in this city of Chicago, Illinois! The radio and the television announce to the public that murdering and killings are taking place continually.

WHEN YE SHALL SEE ALL THESE THINGS!

Today, there is great disrespect of one another!

Mother and her daughter are walking the streets in shame to the public of decent—minded people! They are throwing their clothes aside from their bodies, trying to keep nothing covered, but their shame! And some barely cover their shame!

"As it was in the day of Noah and Lot, so shall it be in the day of the coming of the son of man.

The Son of man comes to judge man and mankind. The day, the day, the day had come!

As Daniel prophesied, (Bible, Dan 9:26, 27) "...and unto the end the war desolations are determined."

"...and for the overspreading of abominations he shall make it desolate, even until the consummation, and that determined shall be poured upon the desolate."

Just think about it! At the end of the war, desolation; so that puts an end to the hope of those who expect to see a great boost of prosperity after the war!

In the day of Noah, the children of the Sodomites came out happy that morning, and that was the end. They saw a cloud making up. They just considered that it was a regular rain cloud, but that was the end!

In the Bible prophecy of Jesus (Matt. 24:38,39). "For as in the days that were before the flood they were eating and drinking, marrying and giving in marriage, until the day that Noah entered into the ark, and knew not until the flood came, and took them all away."

In the time of Noah, the people of Noah were having parties as you are doing today, and that day was the end.

In the time of Sodom and Gomorrah, they were so

wicked that they were willing to go to war with the angels (in the house of Lot).

The Sodomites attacked the angels of God, Who had power to destroy the Sodomites almost instantly. The Sodomites warned that they had been watching the Angels visiting the house of Lot!

A terrible time is gradually approaching upon us. A time so terrible until it will make children grey-headed, the Holy Qur'an teaches us.

The Bible teaches us that it will be a time never witnessed by man and there will be such time in the hereafter. It is a great time. Day and night storms are writhing the country. It is storming day and night!

The Holy Qur'an prophesies of calamities, one right after the other. This we are witnessing with our own eyes. O America, O America, where shall ye flee?

The Holy Qur'an teaches us (Black man) to take refuge in Allah. Today, people laugh at you if you invite them to do righteousness. They make mock of your doing right.

So did the people of Noah and Lot, as it is said so beautifully in Jesus' prophecy, "So shall it be in the day of the coming of the Son of man."

When ye shall see all these things, that you now see, know that it is here; We are living in the end!

My Black people, I say fly to Allah (God) for refuge, and come, follow me. I may look weak, but, through me, you will find refuge in Allah.

CHAPTER 61

The Judgment Nears

Everywhere that we look, and everything that we can think about, marks the end of this world. There never was a time in the history of the United States of America that the President goes out to try to visit the heads of all of the nations that seem to be somewhat his equal!

He is like a criminal who has committed a crime and he hopes for mercy from those whom he has committed the crime against! We cannot escape our doom when it comes, teaches the Holy Qur'an, and the Bible.

They showed no mercy at all to the Black slave. They treated the Black slave worse than any human being has ever been treated. They continue to do so, in the face of divine judgment.

They remind you of the parable of "The Rich Man and the Poor Man." As long as the rich man enjoyed luxury, he cared nothing about luxury for his slave, Lazarus.

Then, at last the rich man fell into poverty and he was unable to get help, even for himself.

The Bible says of the poor Black slave that "none helped them." Now the rich man gets in the place of his once slave. The rich man can witness how it feels to be a poor man.

The parable says, "At last the rich man died. And in hell he lifted up his eyes." He saw his slave in the bosom of Abraham, in the heaven that the slave had been promised that he would get into. It was such a beautiful heaven that the poor slave was lolling around in.

The rich man cried out to the slave to share hell with him. (He asked the slave to bring him a drop of water in hell.) He knew that if the slave tried to get to hell with a drop of water, the slave would never get to heaven.

The rich man would be happy if he received a drop of water to ease his pain and torment. But if the slave could not come to him with a drop of water, then go to some of the rich man's brothers, who the rich man knew were bound to get a taste of the same hell that the rich man was in.

The rich man said, "Father Abraham, if you will not let Lazarus come to me, then send him to my brothers." In words to say, "They are bound to get hell, too."

So, I say to you, the time is not far off. This parable is now in the working. I say to you my Black Brother Lazarus, "Try to stay in the bosom of Abraham," because no man came to us, as the Bible teaches us. No man came to the poor Lazarus (Lost-Found). No one aided him.

I have been begging for help to borrow money saying that we would give the extreme interest. No one has come to our aid yet. The white man has tried to prevent everyone who would give us a little help.

So Allah (God) came to help us from ourselves. May Allah (God) bless us to do his will and bless us to please Him, for Allah (God) is the only help that we have.

I do not care what interest we offered, no one wanted to loan us. They know that we are well worth the loan, but they do not want us to be helped. They figure we are going too fast as it is!

But, O rich man. O rich man! your day has come Your fall has come and no one will help you. They do not want to come near. They see divine destruction licking its tongue about you, on all sides. They do not want to get near to you.

Europe is standing afar, and will not come near. She does not want anything of you. Europe sees your doom and she does not want any herself.

Woe to the white slave-master. "In Hell He Lifted Up His Eyes!"

CHAPTER 62

The Worst is Yet To Come

According to radio and television, and according to individual conversation—and according to conversation heard between government officials concerning their problem of trying to find a way to peace for their people—and a way to find stoppage of the fall of their money market and unemployment—and a stoppage to the revolutions between the dissatisfied and the dissatisfied—and to find a way to be able to eat—and to keep the hungry eating from his own labor—pacification is offered but it does not satisfy.

With nations rejecting peace offers and nations laughing and making mock of you for ever seeking peace and friendship — as it is written, 'Peace is desired more than fine gold!'

Now to see all of these things coming to pass—things that we did not know that we would see. We did not know that we would see such a Goliath—such a giant—falling.

Goliath! who has defied the nations of the earth to come out and fight with them, as Goliath did before Israel. Now, nations make mock of the great giant of the earth, America.

The sword within and the sword without! Trouble seems to have no end. And with tens of millions of free Black slaves crying for freedom, justice and equality from the white slave-master — and the white slave-master wanting to deceive the Black slave and make promises that the white slave-master does not intend to fulfill to his free Black slave—

And with the free Black slave thinking the he will eat some crumbs of freedom, justice and equality from his white slave-master—the free Black slave will be gravely deceived!

The white slave-master cannot free himself from his enemies, not to think of the white slave-master freeing himself from the consequences of the dissatisfied world.

So, with "The Worst Yet To Come," I say to you my Black brothers and my Black sisters, fly to Allah; and come follow me! There are some intelligent white people who know and who will bear witness with me that the worst is yet to come!

Look at Texas! There is a warden at a certain prison-house who sends the believers (Muslims) to the Temple so that they may listen to the truth which is their salvation today; to accept the truth.

I think that this is a very wise warden. It is like Ahab's general (Bible). The general knew that Ahab was wrong and that Elijah was right.

Ahab's general took four hundred of Elijah's followers and hid and fed them with the bread of Ahab in order to save them from hunger while they were in captivity to Ahab.

I say to you leaders, remember the above-said of this writing, that "The Worst Is Yet To Come!" As the Bible teaches us that "a time would come that had never come before," and that those who understood—"their hearts would be failing them with fear and their eyes would go away in their holes" for looking at the things that they saw coming on their people—the trouble! the destruction! and the plagues!

Look at the earthquakes that are taking place. Those earthquakes are on their way here. We are feeling the earth shaking under our feet across the country!

As the Holy Qur'an prophesies to us, "you will hear it coming from distant places with vehement raging and roaring!"

America is beset all around now with troubles and destructions which have happened. America thought that she was immune to the troubles and destructions which are going on in other nations.

Now the same trouble and destruction that you read of as happening in other countries and to other nations—these same troubles and destruction, with their evil and gruesome sound, are knocking on the door of America!

INDEX

258

INDEX

INDEX

INDEX

The
Muslim Program

What the Muslims Believe

1. WE BELIEVE in the One God Whose proper Name is Allah.

2. WE BELIEVE in the Holy Qur-an and in the Scriptures of all the Prophets of God.

3. WE BELIEVE in the truth of the Bible but we believe that it has been tampered with and must be reinterpreted so that mankind will not be snared by the falsehoods that have added to it.

4. WE BELIEVE in Allah's Prophets and the Scriptures they brought to the people.

5. WE BELIEVE in the resurrection of the dead—not in physical resurrection—but in mental resurrection. We believe that the so-called Negroes are most in need of mental resurrection: therefore, they will be resurrected first.

Furthermore, we believe we are the people of God's choice, as it has been written, that God would choose the rejected and the despised. We can find no other persons fitting this description in these last days more than the so-called Negroes in America. We believe in the resurrection of the righteous.

6. WE BELIEVE in the judgment; we believe this first judgment will take place as God revealed, in America...

7. WE BELIEVE this is the time in history for the separation of the so-called Negroes and the so-called white Americans. We believe the black man should be freed in name as well as in fact. By this we mean that he should be freed from the names imposed upon him by his former slave masters. Names which identified him as being the slave master's slave. We believe that if we are free indeed, we should go in our own people's names—the black peoples of the earth.

8. WE BELIEVE in justice for all, whether in God or not; we believe as others, that we are due equal justice as human beings. We believe in

262

What the Muslims Believe

equality—as a nation—of equals. We do not believe that we are equal with our slave masters in the status of "freed slaves".

We recognize and respect American citizens as independent peoples and we respect their laws which govern this nation.

9. WE BELIEVE that the offer of integration is hypocritical and is made by those who are trying to deceive the black peoples into believing that their 400-year-old enemies of freedom, justice and equality are, all of a sudden, their "friends". Furthermore, we believe that such deception is intended to prevent black people from realizing that the time in history has arrived for the separation from the whites of this nation.

If the white people are truthful about their professed friendship toward the so-called Negro, they can prove it by dividing up America with their slaves.

We do not believe that America will ever be able to furnish enough jobs for her own millions of unemployed, in addition to jobs for the 20,000,000 black people as well.

10. WE BELIEVE that we who declared ourselves to be righteous Muslims, should not participate in wars which take the lives of humans. We do not believe this nation should force us to take part in such wars, for we have nothing to gain from it unless America agrees to give us the necessary territory wherein we may have something to fight for.

11. WE BELIEVE our women should be respected and protected as the women of other nationalities are respected and protected.

12. WE BELIEVE that Allah (God) appeared in the Person of Master W. Fard Muhammad, July, 1930; the long-awaited "Messiah" of the Christians and the "Mahdi" of the Muslims.

We believe further and lastly that Allah is God and besides HIM there is no God and He will bring about a universal government of peace wherein we all can live in peace together.

What the Muslims Want

This is the question asked most frequently by both the whites and the blacks. The answers to this question I shall state as simply as possible.

1. We want freedom. We want a full and complete freedom.

2. We want justice. Equal justice under the law. We want justice applied equally to all, regardless of creed or class or color.

3. We want equality of opportunity. We want equal membership in society with the best in civilized society.

4. We want our people in America whose parents or grandparents were descendants from slaves, to be allowed to establish a separate state or territory of their own — either on this continent or elsewhere. We believe that our former slave masters are obligated to provide such land and that the area must be fertile and minerally rich. We believe that our former slave masters are obligated to maintain and supply our needs in this separate territory for the next 20 to 25 years — until we are able to produce and supply our own needs.

Since we cannot get along with them in peace and equality, after giving them 400 years of our sweat and blood and receiving in return some of the worst treatment human beings have ever experienced, we believe our contributions to this land and the suffering forced upon us by white America, justifies our demand for complete separation in a state or territory of our own.

5. We want freedom for all Believers of Islam now held in federal prisons. We want freedom for all black men and women now under death sentence in innumerable prisons in the North as well as the South.

We want every black man and woman to have the freedom to accept or reject being separated from the slave master's children and establish a land of their own.

We know that the above plan for the solution of the black and white conflict is the best and only answer to the problem between two people.

6. We want an immediate end to the police brutality and mob attacks against the so -called Negro throughout the United States.

We believe that the Federal government should intercede to see that

What the Muslims Want

black men and women tried in white courts receive justice in accordance with the laws of the land — or allow us to build a new nation for ourselves, dedicated to justice, freedom and liberty.

7. As long as we are not allowed to establish a state or territory of our own, we demand not only equal justice under the laws of the United States, but equal employment opportunities — NOW!

We do not believe that after 400 years of free or nearly free labor, sweat and blood, which has helped America become rich and powerful, that so many thousands of black people should have to subsist on relief, charity or live in poor houses.

8. We want the government of the United States to exempt our people from ALL taxation as long as we are deprived of equal justice under the laws of the land.

9. We want equal education — but separate schools up to 16 for boys and 18 for girls on the condition that the girls be sent to women's colleges and universities. We want all black children educated, taught and trained by their own teachers.

Under such schooling system we believe we will make a better nation of people. The United States government should provide, free, all necessary text books and equipment, schools and college buildings. The Muslim teachers shall be left free to teach and train their people in the way of righteousness, decency and self respect.

10. We believe that intermarriage or race mixing should be prohibited. We want the religion of Islam taught without hinderance or suppression.

These are some of the things that we, the Muslims, want for our people in North America.